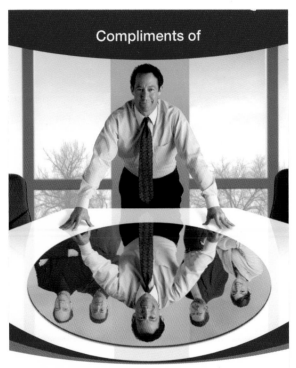

Compliments of

TEC CHIEF EXECUTIVES WORKING TOGETHER | better leaders **decisions** results

THE WORLD'S LEADING CHIEF EXECUTIVE ORGANIZATION

WWW.TEC-CANADA.COM

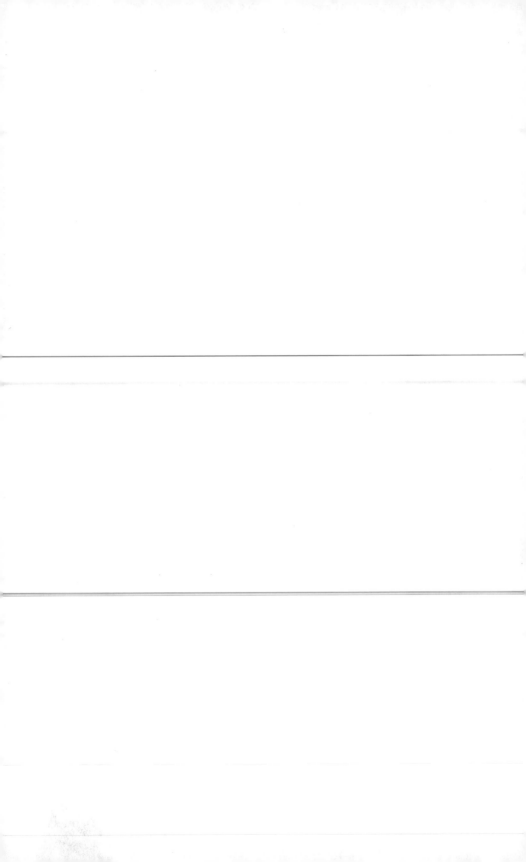

"Nancy Ahlrichs is right-on! Her questions at the end of each chapter are invaluable and challenging discussion subjects to reinforce the learning. A must read for every manager!"

**—SIDNEY TUCHMAN**, PRESIDENT,
TUCHMAN TRAINING SYSTEMS

*Igniting Gen B and Gen V* is a rich, practical resource for tapping the huge reservoir of unused talent you already have in your organization. It's a road map to the level of innovation and creativity that companies need to survive in today's business world."

**—DOUG HICKOK**, PRESIDENT,
HICKOK GROUP, LLC

"A plan to slow or reduce the attrition of Baby Boomers and Veterans is flawed if it does not include a strategy for fully engaging that retained talent so as to capture the full value of their knowledge while contemporaneously transferring it through training to less experienced personnel. This book explains employee engagement and discusses strategies for raising engagement levels within your entire workforce."

**—MARTIN KLAPER**, SENIOR PARTNER,
CAREER DEVELOPMENT OFFICER, ICE MILLER

"*Igniting Gen B and Gen V* is insightful and provides great strategies for energizing all staff at any point in their career and for becoming an employer of choice in our increasingly competitive talent marketplace."

—**ALEX D. OAK, PE,** CHAIRMAN AND CEO, CRIPE ARCHITECTS & ENGINEERS

"Ahlrichs' question-answer style immediately motivates you to question how you can apply the 'five truths that ignite' in your own work situation. Chapter 4 alone makes the book worth buying! Her myth-busters are applicable cross-culturally and globally."

—**MARVINA ANDRUS SHILLING,** PRESIDENT, INTERCULTURAL MANAGEMENT TRAINING & CONSULTING

"Take an inventory of your longtime employees and look at them as if they just started with the company. What career path would you map out for them knowing their strengths and weaknesses? You don't know that with a new employee."

—**TONY DAVIDSON,** PRESIDENT/CEO, KICHLER LIGHTING

"This book will allow you to re-message yourself in ways your employees will applaud and marvel at. The boss really can learn, did hear us and change, and, most important, respects us. That's the gold mine you can tap in this fine read. Invest in your learning!"

—**W. LYNN TANNER, PHD,** PRESIDENT, TEC CANADA

*Igniting Gen B and Gen V*

# igniting

## GEN B & GEN V

### The New Rules of Engagement for Boomers, Veterans, and Other Long-Termers on the Job

## Nancy S. Ahlrichs

**DAVIES-BLACK PUBLISHING**
MOUNTAIN VIEW, CALIFORNIA

Published by Davies-Black Publishing, a division of CPP, Inc., 1055 Joaquin Road, 2nd Floor, Mountain View, CA 94043; 800-624-1765.

Special discounts on bulk quantities of Davies-Black books are available to corporations, professional associations, and other organizations. For details, contact the Director of Marketing and Sales at Davies-Black Publishing: 650-691-9123; fax 650-623-9271.

Visit the Davies-Black Publishing Web site at www.daviesblack.com.

Printed in the United States of America.
11 10 09 08 07 10 9 8 7 6 5 4 3 2 1

**Library of Congress Cataloging-in-Publication Data**

Ahlrichs, Nancy S.
   Igniting Gen B and Gen V : the new rules of engagement for boomers,
   veterans, and other long-termers on the job / Nancy S. Ahlrichs.—1st ed.
      p. cm.
   Includes bibliographical references and index.
   ISBN: 978-0-89106-226-4 (hardcover)
   1. Long-term employees—United States. 2. Employee retention—United States.
   3. Employee motivation—United States. 4. Organizational learning—United States.
   5. Organizational effectiveness—United States.
      I. Title.
   HF5549.5.L66A35 2007
   658.3'14—dc22
                                                                          2007007435
FIRST EDITION
First printing 2007

# • • • • Contents

*To William Haeberle, PhD, professor emeritus,
Kelly School of Business at Indiana University,
who prodded me to consider whether longtime
employees could match the performance of newer
hires; and to Connie Kallback, my cheerleader
and insightful editor at Davies-Black Publishing.*

# • • • • About the Author

Nancy Ahlrichs has more than twenty years of experience in human resources, marketing, and management. As principal of EOC Strategies, LLC, she shares her management, recruiting, retention, and diversity research in her speaking and consulting. Previously she served as Director of Organizational Evolution and as Director of Marketing and Public Relations for ONEX, Inc., an Indianapolis-based high-tech solutions consulting firm with offices in the Midwest. Ahlrichs is author of *Manager of Choice: Five Strategies for Cultivating Top Talent* and *Competing for Talent: Key Recruitment and Retention Strategies for Becoming an Employer of Choice* and a contributor to *On Staffing,* and she has written numerous articles and guest columns for newspapers, journals, and online resources.

Company presidents, CFOs, senior human resources professionals, hospital and other management teams, and even plant managers have found her approach to be both strategic, tactical, and, most of all, practical. Ahlrichs has spoken to hundreds of audiences and management teams in utilities, insurance, health care, high tech, legal, banking, government, and other fields in the past several years.

Governor Frank O'Bannon named Ahlrichs a "Distinguished Hoosier" for her service to the State of Indiana, and she was named "Kiwanian of the Year 2001–2002." A Purdue graduate with both her B.A. and M.S. degrees in anthropology, she is also certified as a Senior Professional in Human Resources (SPHR). Ahlrichs served on the board of directors for a Cleveland-based high-tech human resources software development firm and is active in a variety of community and professional organizations, including the Kiwanis Club of Indianapolis and the Society for Human Resource Management (SHRM). Visit her Web site at www.eocstrategies.com.

# • • • • Introduction

Close your eyes. Picture yourself touring your workplace. Walk through the halls and visit every department. Notice the energy level of the people around you. Count the smiles. Listen for the greetings, ideas, and thank-yous. Ask yourself how you will grow your bottom line if half of your current staff is coasting to retirement and the other half insists on work–life balance.

Now, picture yourself walking from department to department two years from now, after the successful implementation of a process that rewards employee engagement—even the engagement of employees who are nearing retirement. Imagine every employee taking responsibility for innovation: no one resting on his or her laurels or waiting for management's orders. Imagine your best longtime employees requesting new challenges, suggesting ideas, and finding ways to stay beyond their anticipated retirement date. Notice the electricity in the air and the energy of the people around you. Sense the smiles even before you see the faces. Know that this year and going forward, the bottom line is going to improve.

Employee engagement has surfaced as a leading factor in talent management. Traditionally, the focus has been on integrating, motivating and retaining younger employees, while assuming that older, long-time employees will do their job faithfully, but no more, if no less. But that attitude is out of step with reality. Today's competitive marketplace demands that *all* employees do more than their job. Adding to the urgency, Generation X does not have enough members to replace more than 78 million retiring Boomers and Veterans, and too few Generation Y and Z employees have the basic math, spelling, decision-making, and other skills needed for even entry-level positions.

The solution? Increase the number of engaged Boomers and Veterans on staff—and encourage them to skip retirement either part-time or altogether; and encourage retirees to return, by offering alternative work arrangements that enable the best person to perform a specific task while transferring knowledge to the up-and-comers. Today, senior, middle, and HR management need to work together to develop an organization-wide competency in employee engagement. Every manager, every program—such as compensation, benefits, or rewards—and every policy can reinforce this competency.

Your competitive edge will be your organization's ability to consistently draw out the best ideas, best performance, and longest retention of all its employees. This book shows you how to do that starting today.

Chapter 1 explores the magnitude of the engagement deficit in the United States, in other countries, and in your organization.

Chapter 2 delves into the causes of disengagement and begins the process of measuring progress toward reengagement and profitability.

Chapter 3 reveals the five barriers to full engagement now that all employees have job and career choices—the five myths that have acted as unspoken operating rules in most organizations.

Chapter 4 zeros in on the powerful, positive truths that are the foundational beliefs about employees in organizations focused on employee engagement, daily innovation and creativity, and customer satisfaction.

Chapter 5 spotlights the strategies that can be used to capture needed knowledge before it literally walks out the door, and the tactics that will not only minimize knowledge loss but also increase innovation and creativity.

Chapter 6 is a call to action: change the engagement levels of your longtime employees or be left in the dust by your competitors.

As a nation, we face many challenges, but we have the ingenuity, drive, and competitiveness to overcome them. This book is full of examples of companies that have tapped their longtime employees and changed the direction of their fortunes. In the next few years, we will face not only a labor shortage but also a skills shortage. Neither Gen X nor immigration will be able to fill the holes left by knowledgeable retiring employees. This is our wake-up call to change the rules of engagement and maintain our position as a global market leader.

# ENGAGEMENT OR ATTENDANCE?

# Re-ignite Engagement in Longtime Employees

If you are not wearing a watch, hold up your hand. If your watch has a dead battery but you wear it for jewelry, hold up your hand. If you do not intend to replace the battery in your watch when it dies, hold up your hand, too. If your cell phone is your watch, you are not alone. The cell-phone-as-watch-replacement trend may have started with teens and 20-somethings, but it is so rapidly sweeping all generations that many market analysts no longer recommend buying stock in watch companies. In 2005 alone, the $7.1 billion watch market took a 5.5 percent dip.[1]

My 25- and 30-year-old nephews do not own watches, day planners, televisions, or clock radios. They use multifunction devices instead: cell phones, PDAs, laptops, and MP3 players. Who needs heavy, stationary, or redundant equipment when sleek, portable alternatives exist?

Your company's future competition is not your current competition. Welcome to the twenty-first century and the reason employers cannot afford the opportunity cost of letting longtime employees either retire early or coast to retirement. Employers need every employee to have an ear to the ground for the next big thing to affect their business, for the new ways that customers want their needs to be met, and for less-than-obvious competition.

This book is not about the direction of technology. It is about why and how employers must engage and listen to all employees—especially the most productive and customer-focused ones: Baby Boomers and Veterans, the people born before 1965. This book is about delaying the full retirement of productive employees and ramping up their engagement instead of letting them coast into the sunset. For too long, the spotlight has been on the up-and-comers, that narrow slice of high-energy, midcareer employees in their 30s who are skilled and assumed to be responsive to marketplace changes.

I propose that any employee treated like an up-and-comer will respond with 150 percent effort—and the flexibility needed to compete globally today. Your organization's Boomer and Veteran employees would like to be sought out for advice, trained in the latest technology, given high-profile projects, mentored, and expected to be innovative. After twenty-five years of corporate upheaval, longtime employees who are told, "Just do your job. We'll ask if we want your ideas," follow those orders or leave. They have disengaged, but they get up every day to work for an average of $27 per hour. They show up on time, but they leave their brain at the door. Salaried or hourly, too many just do their job—no more, no less. Too many U.S. employers, convinced that the United States will continue to dominate world markets, settle for this meager engagement and productivity.

Rethinking our management approach and utilization of longtime employees is no longer optional. When 77 million Boomers retire, only 56 million Generation Xers will be on hand to replace them.

In other countries, no one is merely showing up. China, India, and Eastern European countries are racing the United States to the top. Their employees are engaged because their job is their ticket to a better life for themselves and their family. Every day, and most nights, 800 million Chinese set out full of personal and national pride to work for less than the equivalent of $5 an hour with the explicit intent to be the number one seller to world markets. In India, where 25 million babies are born annually, people work for somewhat higher wages because their government has been investing in education and technology for more than ten years. Call center work, programming, and design are growth areas. Outsourced manufacturing jobs go to China. Outsourced knowledge jobs go to India. Many other countries are emerging to compete with these two first-comers. When skilled, less expensive talent becomes available elsewhere, even the jobs now outsourced to China and India will hop borders to hungrier, more entrepreneurial workers. It already happened in the 1990s in Mexico, with many U.S.-outsourced manufacturing jobs going overseas instead.

Who is outsourcing to the United States? What edge would they gain if they did outsource to us?

The June 12, 2006, issue of *Newsweek* features a section titled "The Global Leadership Challenge: 15 Ideas for America's Future." The ideas are good: fix our schools, spend more on research, change the culture, view rivals as partners, and so on. The idea with the most immediate impact, however, is one formulated by Mark Warner, former governor of Virginia. Warner says, "We're going to have to draw on ideas all across the spectrum. . . . These challenges demand that we move beyond left versus right and liberal versus conservative. It's got to be future versus past." Indeed, and we need to draw on the ideas of our employees who are beyond the up-and-comer stage.

We in the United States—individuals and businesses—do not seem to realize how fast the industrialized and nonindustrialized world is catching up to us. We cannot rest on our laurels or anything else. No country matches the United States in its ability to attract and retain talent or in its openness to new ideas. We have a tradition of risk taking, innovation, and flexibility, which has powered us to this point. We will never, however, have the sheer volume of labor found in China or India, nor can we match those countries in numbers of graduating engineers. We do have the intellectual capability to create new industries and to remake ourselves in response to the changing world. Global competition is our new Sputnik, and engaged longtime employees are the new up-and-comers.

## DEMOGRAPHICS DO NOT EQUAL DESTINY

The Society for Human Resource Management's "2005 Future of the U.S. Labor Pool" survey of nearly four hundred human resources professionals acknowledged a lack of competencies among new hires:[2]

- Lack of overall professionalism: 59 percent

- Poor writing skills: 58 percent

- Lack of analytical skills: 47 percent

- Poor verbal communication skills: 44 percent

- Lack of business knowledge: 44 percent

This deficit is changing our hiring policies and practices. With the current U.S. unemployment rate below 5 percent, ongoing difficulty finding candidates with the appropriate skills, and the number of long-fill jobs at most organizations, it is critical to retain the best employees of any age and to develop an employment brand that attracts employees with either the needed skills or the capacity and desire to learn them.

Since the 1990s, employers have focused on integrating Gen X and Gen Y hires into the organization. These employees typically leave in one to three years, so the backstop has been Boomers and Veterans, who tend to stay for ten years. See Table 1 for the years that define each generation.

Demographic changes wrought by the pending retirement of long-time employees will exacerbate the skills shortage by drastically reducing the labor pool. Unlike the high-tech labor shortage in the late 1990s, this shortage is multifaceted and expected to last beyond 2020. Simultaneously, 80 percent of the predicted labor shortage will really be a skills shortage.

The oldest Baby Boomers will start retiring in the traditional sense in 2010—though many have been taking early retirement since 2001. While the total size of the U.S. workforce continues to grow, the rate of growth will slide from 12 percent in this decade to only 4 percent per year between 2010 and 2020. By 2020, immigration will account for

| TABLE 1    GENERATIONS IN THE WORKFORCE | |
| --- | --- |
| Veterans | Born before 1946 |
| Baby Boomers | Born 1946–1964 |
| Generation X | Born 1965–1977 |
| Generation Y | Born 1978–1987 |
| Generation Z | Born 1988–2001 |

nearly all of our net workforce growth, and 80 percent of the growth in the native-born workforce will be among employees over age 50.

In the near term, the Employment Policy Foundation estimates that the creation of 23 million net new jobs by 2010 will exceed the supply of new and skilled workers by a wide margin.[3] Add to that the collapse of the skilled labor pool and the result will be a real GDP growth rate of just 2.4 percent from 2011 to 2030 versus 3.3 percent annually averaged in the United States from 1955 to 2006. Europe and Japan will have markedly lower rates of GDP growth because the proportion of retirees to active workers is even more skewed in those countries. This is important because economic performance is based on two things: the size of the workforce and its productivity. A retiring workforce without an adequate skilled replacement is an unwelcome scenario begging to be rewritten.

The "perfect storm" of Baby Boomer retirements, a widening skills gap, and outdated approaches to talent management threaten long-term business performance, according to a survey of nearly 1,400 human resources professionals conducted by Deloitte's Human Capital Practice.[4] Over 70 percent of Deloitte's survey respondents confirmed that they were experiencing and expected to experience a shortage of white-collar employees, and 40 percent said it affected the organization's ability to innovate. Oddly, only 13 percent cited the near-term Boomer retirements as a concern. This shows that we are not in the habit of turning to our over-40-year-olds or our near-retirement-age employees as a source of needed innovation.

Irrespective of the size of the organization, 54 percent of Deloitte's survey respondents said that talent management issues would affect the organization's productivity. Some 30 percent expressed concern about their future ability to meet productivity requirements and fulfill customer demands. One source for relief will be outsourcing, but a 2005 Gartner study found that 80 percent of companies that outsourced customer service functions failed to meet their cost-savings targets.[5] Outside contractors might be more efficient, but they do not identify with the organization—and that can result in frustrated customers who switch to competitors. In-house employees tend to be more interested in nurturing a good reputation among clients and customers.[6] Human resources professionals, backed by senior management and partnering with all hiring managers, need to take action before valuable longtime employees hit the door.

The ongoing skills gap and resulting productivity gap will constrain hiring efforts, according to *Trends*.[7] In the 1960s and 1970s, college-educated Boomers entering the workplace replaced less educated Veteran-generation employees. Today's new workers are no more educated than Boomers. New immigrants tend to have lower education levels than Boomers, though their work ethic is similar to that of Boomers and Veterans. Gains in productivity due to increased education will level off without a significant increase in the education levels of both immigrants and native-born workers.

## NOTE THE OPTIMISTIC SIGNS

Three developing trends—if continued—provide the basis for a more positive outlook:

- Delayed retirement
- Selective immigration
- Offshoring

Wise management of these three strategies will enable real workforce growth rates of 1.2 percent per year through 2025, not the dismal expected 0.3 percent. The balance of the desired 3.0 to 3.3 percent GDP growth rate will be provided by innovation: new business models, the streamlining of current processes, and new technology, according to *Trends*.[8]

For the purposes of this book, I will focus on delayed retirement. When coupled with increasing the engagement of longtime employees, this trend will enable organizations to defy the adage "Demographics determines destiny."

Congress struck down mandatory retirement rules in 1986. Today, 20 percent of Veteran-generation men over age 65 are still working. Many people over age 60 do not feel old because they are more mentally and physically fit than their parents were at the same age. Far more Boomers are expected to choose to continue working into their 70s or even longer, health and employers permitting.

Your best candidates for future openings may already work for you! Greater business continuity can be the outcome of developing internal bench strength through ongoing training, clearly defined opportunities, and even career paths for your longtime employees, not just for new hires and up-and-comers. Remember, Boomer employees tend to stay for ten years while Gen Xers and Gen Ys tend to stay three years or less. With skills training often needed annually, the investment in longtime employees pays off. Retaining skilled, high-quality employees increases productivity; reduces time and money spent on recruiting, orientation, and new hire training; and cements customer relationships. Your customers want to work with your top talent—someone who knows the history of their account.

Only a talent management strategy that re-ignites the engagement and productivity of longtime employees, drives innovation, and differentiates the organization from its competitors will blunt the negative bottom-line effects expected from early and even on-time retirements. If you know the number and location of your retirement-eligible employees, you have the preliminary information you need to take action.

## WHAT DOES ENGAGEMENT LOOK LIKE?

To compete globally on a sustained level, we ask our employees to go beyond their job description nearly every day because of ever-changing customer and organizational needs. Engaged employees are more likely than others to comply—helping others with their workload, taking on additional duties, and making an effort to perform the job more effectively, thereby helping to raise overall productivity. Additionally, engaged employees intend to stay for at least one more year with their employer. This intention alone frees time and mental energy. An engaged employee is not spending time on the job updating résumés or surfing the Internet and applying online for new positions. No mind-share is being used for thinking about looking for a job. An employee who moves from the lowest level of engagement to the highest level of engagement is 87 percent less likely to take a job elsewhere.[9]

The Corporate Leadership Council's 2004 landmark study "Driving Employee Performance and Retention Through Engagement" shows that highly engaged employees experience up to 20 percent better performance and are up to 87 percent less likely to leave their organization.[10] Corporate treatment of employees is the key to increasing engagement levels. The opportunity to boost the bottom line by increasing the percentage of engaged employees is obvious, but too few organizations now focus on the link between engagement and profitability.

## ENGAGEMENT FACTORS DIFFER
## BY LEVEL, SEX, AND COUNTRY

To compete effectively by retaining the highest-performing employees, employers must ensure that workers at every level are engaged—not just at the senior management level. A regular paycheck is no longer enough to ensure top performance.

One-size-fits-all has never really worked for clothing, and it doesn't work with engagement either. The level of employee engagement varies by sex. This matters because your employees probably are not all males or all females. In 2004, ISR, a global employee-research and consulting firm, conducted a survey measuring engagement factors of male and female senior executives as well as male and female middle managers.[11] The survey uncovered major differences between the responses of male and female executives, and also within the same sexes at different levels. See Table 2 for their key motivational drivers.

The level of employee engagement also varies by country. In a global economy, when employers are making decisions about where to out-source and how to motivate their multinational employees across their holdings, different engagement levels matter.

For its 2004 global study of employee engagement ("Creating Competitive Advantage from Your Employees"), ISR surveyed nearly 160,000 employees from more than two hundred companies in the United States and nine other large economies: Australia, Brazil, Canada, France, Germany, Hong Kong, the Netherlands, Singapore, and the United Kingdom.[12] Defining engagement as "the degree to which workers iden-tify with, are motivated by and are willing to expend extra effort for their employer," ISR uncovered a number of significant differences among countries.

Culture is everything. Organizations must adapt to different cultural values and norms when it comes to attracting, motivating, and retaining multinational staff. The same core issues influence engagement in most of the countries studied by ISR, but the relative importance of core issues varied by country. For example,

- **Image:** whether employees believe in the company's products and services (least important among U.S. employees)

- **Career development:** long-term opportunities for growth (most important for U.S. and Australian employees)

- **Leadership:** company maintains high ethical standards and seeks employees' opinions (number two for U.S. and Canadian employees)

- **Empowerment:** degree to which managers encourage employee decision making (number three for U.S. employees)

| TABLE 2 | ENGAGEMENT FACTORS BY SEX AND RANK | |
|---|---|---|
| **RANK** | **FEMALE (PERCENT)** | **MALE (PERCENT)** |
| **Executives U.S.** | Working relationships (14.3) | Career development (19.4) |
| | Customer quality focus (9.5) | Reward (9.7) |
| | Communication (9.5) | Stress, balance, and workload (6.5) |
| | Work tools and conditions (4.8) | Image (3.2) |
| **Middle Managers** | Empowerment (23.8) | Leadership (27.5) |
| | Supervision (19) | Reward (17.5) |
| | Career development (9.5) | Image (15) |
| | Stress, balance, and workload (9.5) | Employment security (5) |

*Note:* ISR surveyed 2,157 males and 731 females in five companies across different industries. Percentages refer to the percentage of key drivers for each group—19.4 percent of the key drivers for males were in the career development category.

## LOOK AT THE BUSINESS BENEFITS OF ENGAGEMENT

In 2004, in response to a growing need expressed by its members to increase both productivity and retention, the Corporate Leadership Council mounted a study of more than 50,000 employees at over 100 employers to uncover the business benefits of engagement.[13]

Engagement is essential for performance and retention. The Council defined *engagement* as "the extent to which employees commit to something or someone in their organization. Engagement can be emotional or rational in nature and can be centered on the employee's job, team, manager or organization."[14] In any organization, engaged employees are the key to meeting or exceeding goals.

The study's findings show that employee engagement has the following overall benefits:

- Discretionary effort levels rise by nearly 60 percent.

- Employee performance improves by up to 20 percent.

- Employees' intent to stay with their organizations increases fivefold.

Earlier studies support these findings. Engaged employees have greater achievement of individual work goals.[15] Several studies positively link employee engagement and intent to stay.[16] The engagement–turnover intention link is also strongly associated with employee satisfaction rates with their immediate supervisors.[17] Managerial talent and employee engagement are strongly correlated.[18] Because the manager sets the stage for an engaged workforce, using employee engagement as the metric for manager selection, development, and recognition becomes more important.

## ENGAGED EMPLOYEES OUTPERFORM LESS ENGAGED PEERS

Intent on determining whether engaged employees have bottom-line impact, in 2004 ISR surveyed 650,000 employees in fifty leading global companies to analyze the relationship between the companies' growth in net income and the engagement level of their employees.[19] Organizations with high levels of employee engagement outperformed industry averages by 6 percent over a twelve-month period, while companies with low levels of employee engagement underperformed industry averages by 9 percent for the same period.

---

### Engagement = Performance = Profits at Owens Corning

After a series of injuries and a death at its plant in Newark, Ohio, Owens Corning brought in David Rabuano to restore smooth operations by engaging employees in the massive turnaround needed. "We are absolutely convinced that there is a competitive edge to be gained by engaging our people through better managed communication," says Dave Brown, CEO of the Toledo-based company. "We have seen it pay off already in measurable improvements in costs and productivity."

After building engagement among employees, one upstate New York Owens Corning plant increased production by 12 million pounds while cutting costs by $2 million and substantially reducing injuries. Rabuano reports overall results of $15 million of increased sales volume in one year and a 76 percent decline in accidents. "We see a lot more smiles on faces," he says.[20]

---

Other studies back up these findings.[21] Research shows that engaged employees are likely to have reduced turnover, absenteeism, and accidents and higher customer loyalty, profitability of sales per employee, market value, and gross return on capital than those employees who are not engaged.[22]

## IT'S TIME FOR COORDINATED ACTION

Business strategies are becoming people-dependent, focusing more on customer satisfaction than on cost management. Customers demand engaged employees who can deliver faster, cheaper, better products and services. Re-igniting engagement and extending the work span of nearly half of current employees may be the fastest way to deliver on customer expectations and remain competitive. Clearly, simply bringing in new hires to boost productivity is not working because the new hires' skills and behaviors require large training investments to bring them up to speed.

Will Rogers got it right: "Even if you're on the right track, you'll get run over if you just sit there." If economic performance is based on two things—the size of the workforce and its productivity—and if the workforce is shrinking and engaged employees are the most productive, then every organization must focus on extending the work span of its longtime employees and increasing individual engagement. In the United States, nearly 50 percent of workers are in the Baby Boomer or Veteran generation. Their "early to arrive, late to leave" work ethic has been counted on to hold organizations together through mergers, acquisitions, product and process changes, zero defects campaigns, Six Sigma, gas shortages, and every other crisis in U.S. business. As the workhorses of the workforce, longtime employees have been assumed to be self-winding.

To achieve organizational goals and thrive when tomorrow's competition may not even come from your industry sector (cell phones as watch replacements, for example)—much less your part of the globe—senior management can no longer simply demand an undefined "more" from employees.

In the United States, where too many employees forgo vacation days each year, no one can give more time without burning out. Doing "more with less" has moved from cliché to impossibility as there is less "less" available. Customers demand unique solutions and cost-conscious creativity. "More" must be redefined for each employee's role.

Engagement is the opposite of burnout. Engaged employees wake up happy on Mondays. They *expect* to do more than their job description requires. They aren't coasting to retirement or any other destination because they feel connected to results today and the possibility of innovation and achievement tomorrow.

Only a coordinated talent management strategy crafted by HR and implemented by every level of management will engage employees' discretionary efforts and deliver on senior management's demand for the elusive "more."

## Leverage Longtime Employees

- **For HR:** What percentage of your employee population will be eligible to retire each year through 2020? The analysis will pay off in valuable insight. Does your organization have any departments or branch offices that will lose the majority of employees to retirement in a one-year period? If so, what is your strategy to minimize the negative impact to the organization?

- **For senior management and HR:** What is your organization's business strategy? Is there a talent management strategy to ensure achievement of overall business goals? If not, what are the gaps?

- **For all managers and HR:** Like recruitment, retention is a one-to-one activity. What is your organization's plan to encourage longer work spans among your longtime top talent individuals? What are you personally doing to ensure that your longtime top talent staffers know their options and feel welcome to continue with the organization well into the future?

• • • •

2

# • • • • Reap What You Reward

Woody Allen says, "Eighty percent of life is just showing up." Unfortunately, many companies have that philosophy about employees, the work that they do, and their reward systems. We reward attendance and longevity but skimp on rewarding continuous learning, innovative customer solutions, and asking the question, Why? Every system is perfectly designed to deliver the results it gets. "Showing up" might have been enough when the majority of jobs required repetition, but it is not enough today.

Each decade has a customer-driven theme. The 1980s were about quality. The 1990s were about value and efficiency. The first decade of this century is about productivity and innovation. If you happen to have a large number of employees who are productive and innovative, all the better—but, chances are, you are doing more with less. Today, organizational success can be the outcome even with part-time, telecommuting, or off-site employees, as long as they are engaged and listening to the customers.

According to Margaret M. Blair, nonresident senior fellow at the Brookings Institution, up to 85 percent of a company's value in a knowledge-based economy involves intangible assets such as employee quality (number of degreed associates, levels of training, number of patents, and so on) and productivity.[1] A company whose employees can only be counted on to show up and do their specific job is not worth much. Can you reliably depend on your employees for more than attendance?

Global competition is driving the need to increase productivity while lowering costs. In the United States, this pressure to do more with less has often been translated into RIFs, cuts to training and development, and the offshoring of jobs. Because emerging economies can employ more workers for less money, it is important in industrialized economies for fewer, higher-paid, workers to increase output with a high value of goods. In countries with higher labor costs, only goods and services of higher value can override the advantage of lower labor costs in emerging economies. Higher-value goods and services tend to be developed, perfected, and produced by top talent.

Top talent outperforms average talent by 50 to 100 percent, according to McKinsey's "Value of Better Talent" research reported in *The War for Talent*.[2] Average talent does everything listed in their job description. Top talent routinely does more. It's not how many employees you keep; it's which ones you keep. Among your longtime employees are many obvious A players. Some are less obvious B+ players—B players with A player capabilities. Just ask them! All it will take to turn them into consistent A players is to focus on engagement factors. Whether called top talent or A players, engaged longtime employees are the ones to keep.

The United States is experiencing a "brain drain" of its own. In 2006, two workers were leaving the workforce for every new one entering. By 2008, the employee shortage will top 10 million workers across the United States. Ironically, organizations have been reducing head count for more than twenty years and simultaneously depleting loyalty and engagement among the survivors as well as among future generations of hires. Brain drain occurs when an employee with needed knowledge leaves. It also occurs when remaining knowledgeable employees are disengaged, leave their brain at the door, and just do their job.

Employee retention has become a written goal for managers in many organizations—but retention alone is not a solution to meeting customer needs and organizational growth goals. The keepers will come in all shapes and sizes: some will not be able to work full-time, others will. The key is to keep the engaged employees and to rekindle engagement in as many other employees as possible, whether retirement is five or fifteen years away. Engaged employees who innovate or go above and beyond when responding to customer needs are the only sustainable competitive advantage for any organization. Nordstrom knew this first.

Engaged employees listen to customers and do whatever it takes to meet their needs. They use their discretionary effort. The need for engaged employees who are capable of innovation puts the HR function and its tools—training, recruiting, talent management, benefits management, and the rest—at the center of the competitive drive to create value through intangible assets: people's outlook and behavior.

This chapter focuses on developing a culture that gets the results needed today.

## DO YOU REWARD ATTENDANCE OR ENGAGEMENT?

Organizations get what they reward—and what they permit. Unfortunately, many organizations focus only on attendance and job satisfaction, ignoring engagement and productivity. They have policies, goals, and metrics around the former but not the latter. Attendance requirements and punishment for tardiness frequently lead the list of company policies, and they are covered in the first minutes of orientation. In fact, the overemphasis on attendance can become a barrier to employees' use of discretionary effort. And job satisfaction alone is simply not a state that is related to either retention or productivity.

Examples of this skewed focus abound. In an effort to ease the workload of a small number of employees in the payroll department, many companies have adopted technology-based attendance systems that require logging in and out four times a day: on arrival, when leaving for and returning from lunch, and at the end of the day. With great flourish, these automated attendance systems are introduced to replace allegedly antiquated paper time cards that took five minutes to fill out on a weekly basis. The result? Four times a day, hourly employees are reminded that they are under more scrutiny than their salaried co-workers—so engagement and willingness to take extra time with a task diminish. Clocking in and out on time becomes paramount. Now logging their attendance takes twenty minutes per week instead of five. While fair pay for true hours worked is the obvious goal, an additional outcome is that the organization now has an army of clock-watchers who are merely present. By adding an attendance-focused activity twenty times a week, management sends a clear message: well-documented presence trumps all else. If you don't believe it, ask the affected employees.

Employee satisfaction as an organizational metric is another red herring. According to the 2005 "Walker Loyalty Report for Loyalty in the Workplace," which summarized survey results from more than 2,500 full-time and part-time U.S. employees at companies with at least fifty employees, even the just-described employees are satisfied with their job.[3] They would not change their job content. They show up on time and do their job, but the majority of these employees do not exhibit the additional behaviors an organization needs to keep it competitive and profitable into the future.

In the Walker study, 75 percent of the respondents said that they are satisfied with their job—but only 34 percent are also *truly loyal* and only 6 percent are *accessible*.[4] These two groups recommend their employing organization as a good place to work, resist offers, and are willing to do things beyond their job description. Truly loyal employees (whether hourly or salaried) can envision themselves working for their current employer for at least two more years, while accessible employees would like to make that commitment but have a life circumstance that prevents them (such as a spouse who is frequently transferred, a pregnancy, or the like). Further, truly loyal and accessible employees tend to participate in six strategic activities:

- 360-degree feedback
- Career planning

- Training classes

- Mentor programs

- Job description review

- Promotions

Truly loyal and accessible employees, according to the Walker survey, do more than show up on time and do their job.[5] They ensure that their skills are current in alignment with marketplace changes and customer needs. These are the longtime employees to keep. Expanding their ranks should be the manager's goal—not just retention of as many employees as possible.

Even though they say they are satisfied, 28 percent of Walker's salaried and hourly respondents are classified as *trapped*. Trapped employees would leave if they could—but, for a variety of reasons, are reluctant or unable to do so. They arrive on time, leave on time, and do their job in between. They carry "You want it when?" mugs and post signs that say, "This is a job, and only a job. If this were a real career, I would actually care." They take no risks, ask no questions, and do just enough to not get fired. They are the living dead—and they are killing your organization's brand by delivering the minimum to your customers. Attitudes affect behavior. Attitudes are contagious.

The remaining 31 percent of respondents are deemed *high risk:* they are conducting a job search right now. The only good news is that the next one you lose might be replaced with an enthusiastic truly loyal employee. See Figure 1.

Clearly, job satisfaction does not predict retention—and matters little to the bigger need for engagement, productivity, innovation, and creativity.

As expected, more than a third of longtime employees have high levels of much-needed loyalty (see Figure 2). Note, however, that among those with twenty years of employment with their organization, 31 percent are trapped (would leave if they could) and 25 percent are high risk (conducting a job search). Among those with ten to nineteen years of employment, a whopping 41 percent are trapped and 24 percent are high risk. This means that 65 percent are not truly loyal or engaged.

**FIGURE 1 • LIMITED LOYALTY IN TODAY'S WORKFORCE**

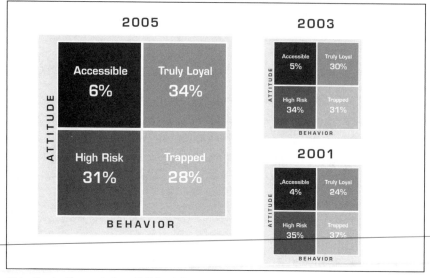

*Note:* Used with permission of Walker Information.

**FIGURE 2 • LOYALTY BY TENURE IN COMPANY**

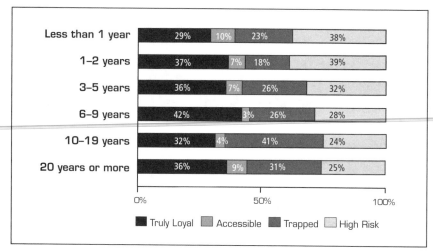

*Note:* Used with permission of Walker Information.

These results are echoed by the findings of a 2005 MetLife Foundation/Civic Ventures study of one thousand U.S. citizens aged 50 to 70.[6] The study, called "New Face of Work Survey," revealed that half the people in the United States aged 50 to 70 say they are interested in taking a job now or in the future to help improve the quality of life in their community. So 50 percent hope to move up, move over, or otherwise change their current responsibilities.

Both the Walker study and the MetLife/Civic Ventures study show that at least half of longtime employees are on the job, but that is all. While senior management assumes that these longtime employees will stay to the end, many are actually devoting every spare minute to conducting active job searches. Many more have quit on the job because they are devoting every spare minute to imagining what it would be like to work elsewhere. This is on-site brain drain. Whether trapped or high risk, these longtime employees want to work—just not where they are currently employed. For an organization to have the majority of its most-trained, most-customer-savvy employees just showing up cannot fail to have a tremendous negative impact on productivity and customer satisfaction. Disengaged employees who merely have good attendance and fulfill the requirements of their outdated job description will not help to move the organization forward.

## WANTED: A CULTURE OF PRODUCTIVITY AND INNOVATION

Organizations cannot cost-cut their way to competitiveness and long-term success. Operating with as little waste as possible is important, but it is not the key to sustainable success. Quality, value, and efficiency are still in demand by customers, but even together, they no longer provide a competitive edge. Driving profits by creating a culture of productivity and innovation is the key to competitive advantage today. Customers want customization at no additional cost and with no delay. Only engaged employees in an organization that places a high value on productivity and innovation will deliver, no matter what stage of their career. The current culture of mere attendance must be replaced!

Innovation and productivity are not accidental occurrences. Systematic people practices central to the cultural fabric at Nokia, Cirque du Soleil, Google, Pixar, and other organizations ensure that all employees focus the majority of their mind-share on what matters to their customers. All employees—including near-retirement employees (and their managers)—are expected to be creative and in tune with current needs and future possibilities.

Every employee has a responsibility to contribute. No coasting is allowed in a culture of productivity and innovation. HR and senior management lead the culture through expectations and practices like these from day one:

- Hiring and retaining innovative and productive employees

- Motivating and recognizing innovative and productive employees

- Developing all employees with innovation and productivity as the end goals

- Selecting managers with a track record of innovation and productivity, and rewarding them for developing both outcomes in their employees

- Keying performance management from innovation and productivity metrics

- Rewarding productive innovators at all levels, in all functions

In a culture of productivity and innovation, every program and process must be aligned with the organization's strategic goals. Every employee is expected to deliver continuous productivity and innovation. According to Scott Cawood and Rita Bailey,[7] in their engagement-focused book, *Destination Profit*, doing away with the "stagnent quo" is the only way to get today's desired results from individual employees.

## FAILURE TO INNOVATE IS NOT AN OPTION

If only engaged employees can deliver innovation and productivity, then a good approach is to determine your organization's current baseline level of employee engagement. In Chapter 1, engagement was defined as an employee's willingness to

- Go beyond their job description
- Help others with their workload
- Take on additional duties
- Make an effort to perform the job more effectively
- Stay on for at least one more year

Combined with the similar efforts of others, these characteristics effectively raise overall productivity. The management of engagement must be integrated into the strategic planning process, focusing resources and attention where engagement has strategic importance. How can an organization measure the engagement level of employees? Survey them—regularly.

Engagement drivers are those elements that senior and middle management and HR can influence if survey scores drop. In each department, different engagement drivers will need attention. Drivers include

---

### Engagement = Performance = Profits at Intuit

Intuit's CEO, Steve Bennett, believes that engaged employees provide quality customer service, share knowledge, innovate to address customer needs, increase product quality, reduce costs, improve processes, and have high productivity and other behaviors needed for strong financial performance.

Intuit regularly surveys its employees relative to its strategic goals and finds that the responses to four agree/disagree points drive the most variation in engagement levels:

- I am proud to work at Intuit.
- Overall, my satisfaction with Intuit is high.
- I would recommend Intuit as a great place to work.
- If offered a similar position and compensation at another company, I would stay at Intuit.[8]

career goals, learning opportunities, total compensation, trust in business unit decision making, and the like. The key is to focus on those drivers most important to alignment with business strategy and to design and execute action plans to close specific gaps. Administering surveys without providing action plans and timely responses will only accelerate disengagement.

Increased discretionary effort and decreased turnover are the rewards when an organization improves workforce engagement. An organization's treatment of its employees has the greatest impact on engagement, creating both opportunities and challenges. The biggest challenge is that engagement is not a group activity. Like recruitment, engagement happens one employee at a time. While the majority of employees appreciate broad initiatives such as surveys, improved communication, benefits options, flextime, organization-wide celebrations, and a fun atmosphere, none of these measures can substitute for satisfactory daily interactions with one's manager. Further, the barriers to full engagement (discussed in Chapter 3) also must be removed for employees to volunteer their discretionary effort.

Marcus Buckingham and Curt Coffman mounted one of the largest analyses of survey data in history and found the questions that discriminate between the most productive departments and wannabes. They uncovered what they call "the Q12" and were able to prove, by looking at their results across 2,500 business units at 24 companies, that engaged employees do indeed drive positive business outcomes.[9] Peculiarly, the Q12 actually includes thirteen questions.

The business units whose employees responded most positively to the Q12 also posted higher productivity, profit, employee retention, and customer satisfaction. Scored on a five-point scale, where 5 is extremely satisfied and 1 is extremely dissatisfied, the majority of the questions are connected to productivity. Each of the questions links to at least one of these four outcomes, while most link to multiple outcomes.

This proprietary list of questions not only reveals which driver of engagement is faltering, it provides very clear instruction to the manager as to the action needed to improve engagement. Different departments and managers will need to work on different drivers to improve productivity in their work groups.

## IT'S TIME FOR COORDINATED ACTION

"If you're early, you're on time. If you're on time, you're late. If you're late, you're dead," according to an old saying. Being there was most important in the past, but the quality of outputs trumps attendance today. Business is moving at warp speed. We use many types of technology to "be there." Providing the services and products that customers want, when and where they want them, requires more than attendance and longevity. It requires engaged employees focused on innovation and productivity.

Engaged employees are the only sustainable competitive advantage. No organization can expect different outcomes tomorrow without making changes to the system that is reinforcing what it is getting today. No organization can experience improved productivity and engagement among longtime employees without their input about those cultural elements that interfere with productivity and without their ideas for innovation. Plan on conducting annual surveys and providing quarterly action plans for individual managers as well as business units. Receiving regular feedback about engagement will enable managers to provide regular course correction, wherever needed. Waiting two years or more between surveys will not provide timely information and could actually become yet another disengagement factor to remove. Without surveys and focus groups to discuss courses of action, many disengagement factors are effectively hidden. If you don't know it's broken, you can't fix it.

## Leverage Longtime Employees

- **For all managers and HR:** In your organization, at what point do new hires first hear about meeting customer needs, productivity, and innovation? At what point do new hires hear about attendance? What does your Web site have to say about these priorities?

- **For HR:** What is your organization's strategy to rekindle engagement among longtime employees? What actions have been taken to date? What results have been noted?

- **For HR:** What percentage of your organization's longtime employees participate in these strategic activities:

  - 360-degree feedback
  - Career planning
  - Training classes
  - Mentor programs
  - Job description review
  - Promotions

- **For senior management and HR:** How are managers held accountable for the continuous development of their longtime employees? Are managers rewarded for going above and beyond in the development of their people?

• • • •

# 3

# • • • • Reject Barriers
# to Full Engagement

What is the cutoff age for a "late bloomer"? There isn't one. The oldest man and woman to complete a marathon are Dimitrion Yordandis, 98, and Jenny Wood-Allen, 91. Forty-three percent of U.S. marathon runners were over age 40 in 2005. Twenty percent of the runners who finished the Boston Marathon in 2006 were age 50 or older. Baby Boomers are making their mark in the sport.[1]

What is the difference between these marathon runners and your longtime employees? Expectations: theirs and yours. If we expect to complete a marathon, we rearrange our routine to include training and discussions with other marathoners so that we learn the tricks to doing it safely and well. We consume a diet that provides the right foods for sustained energy. We surround ourselves with people who urge us on.

For years, no one could crack the four-minute mile—and some said it was impossible. Then Roger Bannister, a 25-year-old British medical student, did it in 1954. After that, many runners broke his record. Whether we expect ourselves or others to break a speed record, run a marathon, or be innovative and creative after age 40, we get what we expect every day.

Traditionally, senior management combs the ranks of the company's up-and-comers (typically under age 40) for potential fast-track employees. HR nudges these employees' managers to ensure that they get stretch assignments, training, and promotions. However, it is the very rare employer that offers all employees over age 40 advanced technology training, cross-training for multiple positions, tuition reimbursement to go back to school, stretch assignments, projects to lead, promotions with or without relocation, or other intensely focused learning experiences. No wonder job content change and organization-wide change are so tough for the majority of longtime employees. No one has expected them to flex their learning muscles.

Interestingly, research from Yale University, Johns Hopkins, and elsewhere shows that people over age 50 who engage regularly in physical training gain muscle strength and improve their performance, relative to their potential, faster than people in their 20s. It is easier for Boomers to slow their biological clock than it is for much younger people.[2] That is energizing just to think about!

Re-igniting engagement works the same way. Longtime employees who are given the tools to stay competitive can make significant contributions relative to their position well past age 40. Employees who receive positive expectations, ongoing skills training, and knowledge of industry trends remain intellectually stimulated, productive, and in a state of discovery. When employees are given tools plus high expectations, they deliver results. Perceptions become reality—or people leave for a job that is a better fit.

The paradox, according to David C. Forman, chief learning officer at the Human Capital Institute, is that too much talk and not enough action inhibits organizations' ability to compete in the talent wars. His research shows that many leaders say they value their human capital and the development of it—but they slip back into command-and-control mode when under pressure.[3] Command-and-control management kills engagement and innovation.

# FIVE MYTHS INHIBIT PERFORMANCE

Command-and-control management isn't the only problem; a number of other factors also discourage engagement. This chapter focuses on the business myths that create disengaged longtime employees.

## Myth 1: I Am [You Are] Too Old

If Boomers did not invent ageism, they perfected it. Boomers grew up saying, "Never trust anyone over 30." Then, when they turned 30, they started the trend to redefine age. Bob Dylan predicted this phenomenon in his song "Forever Young."[4] Television shows, marketers, and clothing designers focus on 18- to 34-year-olds. All of the cachet is on the side of youth. Today, 60 is the new 40 and 55 is the new 35. No one wants to be considered mature, middle-aged, old, older, or over the hill.

Bias is bias, whether it is open or covert. It is destructive for employees and, in addition to being illegal, robs organizations of otherwise capable employees. One of the most insidious outcomes is that the targeted individuals often assume that the generalizations about them must be true.

Jonathan A. Segal, a partner with the Philadelphia-based law firm of Wolf, Block, Schorr, and Solis-Cohen, says that many employers are clearly guilty of what he calls the "Dracula complex." "They want newer and fresher blood, because they're under the mistaken impression that it can bring vitality to an organization," he says. "However, experience and research show us that vitality, productivity and creativity are not age-related at all." He points out that stereotypes like "older workers are slow learners" or "some people are just stuck in their ways" can be just as hurtful as descriptors such as being "stable" or "dependable" or even "loyal."[5] The latter hold no connotation of innovation or creativity.

Negative assumptions about how quickly employees will learn, how willing they are to learn, and how long the organization will benefit from investing in training a longtime employee are just that: assumptions. Too easily, our negative assumptions can undermine aspirations—those of others as well as our own—especially when we set the bar too low. The best organizations value differences—including age—and use differences to build stronger, more diverse, and more competitive services and products.

## Myth 2: Our Employees Know They Are Our Most Important Asset

After twenty-five years of dealing with corporate turmoil, training budget cuts, hands-off management, endless paid or unpaid overtime, shrinking development opportunities, being passed over for promotions, and being taken for granted as "dependable workhorses," longtime employees do not feel that they are considered important assets.

Employees who feel unappreciated are more likely to quit and drive up your organization's recruiting and training costs. Alternatively, they may stay but exhibit other signs of feeling unappreciated: absenteeism, tardiness, low morale and productivity, stress injuries, and union organizing. The value of engaged employees is incalculable. The cost of unappreciated, disengaged employees to U.S. employers is billions of dollars annually.

---

### Engagement = Performance = Profits at Sensis

By focusing on employee engagement, Sensis, an advertising and search company, moved from a sluggish and individualistic culture producing poor profits and enduring 45 percent employee turnover to an inspiring, responsive, and agile organization with a new brand and improved organizational growth. To accomplish this task, the CEO launched a longtime employee engagement initiative with two specific goals: to ensure corporate success in terms of superior profits, and to result in significant, measurable improvement in organizational health. Three years later, surveys showed that 85 percent of the staff understood the company's business, 80 percent felt supported to initiate innovative solutions to work-related problems, and 82 percent reported being engaged in the business.[6]

---

## Myth 3: The Best Ideas Come from Outside the Organization

Many organizations spend tens of thousands of dollars on consultants who regularly contact clients, prospects, vendors, and ex-clients for their feedback and ideas. They use the Internet, focus groups, surveys, cocktail parties, and even cash to coax ideas from outsiders.

Many employers solicit new hires' perspectives on processes and other improvements—and then cease to ask them anything. After about two years, the honeymoon is over. Longtime employees simply are not asked, or they are just given the opportunity to drop suggestions into a box that might as well be poised over a shredder.

The assumption is that the new hire has been "out there" in contact with trends and different ideas, but after even a short period as an employee, she or he conforms to the existing culture and ceases to have any worthwhile observations. Once this happens, offering suggestions and ideas is considered taboo. "Rocking the boat," "sticking your neck out," and otherwise taking chances by speaking up with new ideas will result in frowns, selective deafness on the part of management, and even job loss. Yes, the squeaky wheel often gets the boot.

## Myth 4: The Best Way to Manage People Is to Treat Them All Alike

Longtime employees dread hearing, "If I do it for you, I have to do it for everyone. No exceptions." Too often, managers ignore the eroding engagement levels of Boomer and Veteran employees in favor of spending time with more vocal Gen X and Gen Y employees. While Gen Xers and Gen Ys will quit if the management style chafes them, longtime employees will stay but will fall into the trapped category. Remember, trapped employees do their job but would leave if they could. Mass management is a big mistake in an increasingly individualistic world. "Have it your way" is how most employees want their work life as well as their hamburgers. A steep price is being paid for the disengagement of half or more of the employees in many companies.

**Lack of Engagement = Lack of Profits at Ford Motor Company**

In spite of winning diversity awards—Ford was recognized in 2006 as one of the top American corporations on DiversityInc's list of Top 50 Companies for Diversity as well as named in *Latina Style* magazine's list of fifty best companies for Latinas to work for in the United States—too little employee input too late may have contributed to its low profits. The headlines read "Ford taps employees for ideas" in January 2006—when all other outside sources of ideas had been exhausted.[7] When a company seeks national coverage for an initiative, senior management is serious. Even so, employees were asked to respond via a postage-paid response card attached to a brochure mailed to their home.

The generation of innovative ideas is an active individual endeavor. Passive approaches get passive responses. A cattle call is not effective for recruiters in search of top talent and is unlikely to bring out the best ideas from employees. Suggestion boxes languish if they are irregularly checked and the contents infrequently acknowledged. The response to this direct mail request must have been underwhelming since the company continued to struggle. By November of the same year, almost half of the automaker's U.S. factory workforce—a total of 38,000 employees—had accepted buyout offers to leave the company.[8]

Every organization is challenged with inspiring greater productivity—and engagement—from each employee. One-size management styles and corporate policies are not effective anymore. While Gen Xers and Gen Ys may have been able to negotiate exceptions (flextime, more vacation time, updated laptops, and so on) when they joined the company, longtime employees are finding that leaving may be their only option if they cannot continue to do the same job during the same hours or under the same conditions.

The steady productivity of longtime employees has been taken for granted because of their workhorse habits. These habits are changing as Boomers and Veterans need to cut back their hours and restructure their work arrangements with their employers. Longtime employees may have new issues: elder care, grandchild care, a desire to finish or start a degree, or other needs that require a rethinking of their current work configuration. They may request flextime, telecommuting, part-time, or other work arrangements. Smart managers give flexibility to get engagement and retention. They have discovered that granting exceptions in exchange for requiring high performance is win-win-win for the employee, the manager, and the organization.

Managers of choice—managers who have the most productive employees—know that engagement, productivity, and retention happen one person at a time.

## Myth 5: If Employees Would Just Do Their Job, Everything Would Be Fine

Most employees understand what they are hired to do. They can recite their responsibilities and any schedule that goes along with them. Every day, however, we actually hope employees will do *more* than their job: help others, find new ways to please a disgruntled customer, meet an unplanned deadline, keep costs down, or deal with the unexpected.

If employees do not know the overall strategy of the organization, their work world is twenty feet around their workspace. They cannot contribute suggestions to enhance their individual alignment with the greater organization's goals. They cannot see how their individual performance makes a difference. They can do their job but still be unable to see why a change is worth the extra effort. Worse, "It's not my job" could be the quantifiable truth.

Chances are, your employees are doing their job—but the job is no longer designed to meet today's marketplace or customer demands. The description is often so specific that there is no built-in flexibility to respond to new customer needs or to encourage innovation. Old job descriptions are not going to help deliver on your organization's customer promise if they do not include deliverables for specific customers or any reference to completing the work using the values of the organization. Without a regular review of job descriptions, out-of-date processes and procedures live on and prevent what is needed now.

### Engagement = Performance = Profits at Genecor

"There is a philosophy here of supporting an employee's entire lifestyle because it will make for a better employee and facilitate productivity, which it does," according to Cynthia Edwards, Genecor's vice president of technology.[9]

The Palo Alto–based 1,260-employee company focuses on development and manufacturing of health care products and enzymes. Sales are $380 million a year. Turnover is less than 4 percent—when the national average for the industry is 18.5 percent. The company also generates approximately $60,000 more revenue per employee than its largest competitor, Novozymes.

Ranked in the top five among best medium-sized companies to work for by the Great Place to Work Institute and the Society for Human Resource Management, Genecor sought its employees' input on

- **Environment.** Employees helped to design the new headquarters.

- **Camaraderie.** Employees get to know others in different departments during weekly themed cocktail parties and participation in one or more company clubs.

- **Wellness and fitness.** Employees can take part in sports teams after hours or yoga and aerobics classes during the day.

- **Lifestyle.** Employees save time on errands by taking advantage of on-site travel support, dry cleaning, oil changes, and photo processing.

## IT'S TIME FOR COORDINATED ACTION

Stereotypes and assumptions can no longer guide policies; conversations; decisions about hiring, compensation, and promotions; or strategic business planning. As a country, we face the toughest competition for markets we have ever faced—and we already have a shortage of employees and skills. If Baby Boomers are the trusted, reliable workhorses, why aren't they among the first ones consulted about new approaches for processes, new products and services, and customer service? Why do vendors have more access to senior management to share their ideas than do employees who have invested the prime years of their life in the company and who listen to its customers every day? If your organization's culture does not include expectations, recognition, or mechanisms for longtime employees to contribute to the strategic goals of the organization, you have an unnecessarily short runway for getting your future products and services off the ground.

---

### Leverage Longtime Employees

- **For all managers and HR:** Which of the five business myths has the greatest negative effect on your longtime employees' productivity and innovation?

- **For all managers and HR:** What additional myths came to mind as you read this chapter?

- **For HR:** What cultural elements in your organization perpetuate these myths?

- **For senior management and HR:** What needs to happen to rewrite the myths at your organization?

• • • •

# RETENTION OR RESULTS?

4

# • • • • Release Full Engagement

Like recruitment, engagement happens one heart, one mind at a time. Which of your competitors are already tapping into their longtime employees for ideas, innovations, creativity, or new angles on customer satisfaction? Whose sales are going up?

What skills, experience, and energy—not to mention innovation and creativity—are organizations denying themselves when the majority of former up-and-comers are quietly excluded from training, stretch assignments, and promotions with or without relocation? It is a safe bet that employers underestimated the late-career potential for significant contributions from these people:[1]

- Robert Chambers (62, of Lebanon, New Hampshire), who founded a nonprofit that negotiates fair car prices for the working poor and offers them loans. In the past five years, he has underwritten $10 million in loans.

- June Simmons (64, of San Fernando, California), whose nonprofit organization trains social workers to reduce life-threatening errors for their elderly clients.

- Charles Dey (75, of Lyme, Connecticut), who places disabled high school students in paid internships that provide a workplace mentor.

- Scott Fisher (60), Lou Smit (71), and Charlie Hess (79)—all retired cops who volunteer their time to solve cold cases. After four years of patient conversation, Hess persuaded a killer in prison since 1995 to provide information on forty-eight additional slayings.[2]

- Sidney Sidor (78, of Indianapolis, Indiana), who left "heavy corporate industry" including stints at General Motors and Rockwell International—where he was a chemical and metallurgical engineer, plant manager, and human resources manager—to become a Catholic priest at age 76.[3]

The energy, effort, and creativity exhibited by these mature individuals could be undergirding—or even leading—the product development or customer service efforts at for-profit organizations. This chapter explores five truths—actually, five mind shifts—you can use to re-ignite the full engagement and profitable contribution of your longtime employees.

## FIVE TRUTHS IGNITE PERFORMANCE

Myths have misguided human expectations for centuries. For example, in George Washington's day, the tomato was thought to be poisonous and to be avoided at all costs. Today, we know it is a source of lycopene, a potent nutritional antioxidant. The truth is, tomatoes actually contribute to health!

Engagement is a process, not an event, led by myth-buster managers. Every organization and every manager has the power to re-ignite performance in longtime employees if they will first overturn the misguided beliefs that waste the potential contributions of much-needed longtime employees:

- I am [or, more often, you are] too old.

- Our employees know they are our most important asset.

- The best ideas come from outside the organization.

- The best way to manage people is to treat them all alike.

- If employees would just do their job, everything would be fine.

The CEO alone cannot lead the organization to profits by simply articulating the vision. Managers can also lead by making the vision real to their employees. Further, managers must open the door to new contributions, especially from longtime employees. Without employees who understand their role in making the organization a success, the organization will lose to the competition.

Next, managers must understand that just as top talent is available *outside* the organization, it is also available *inside* the organization—but not every employee has what it takes to propel the organization forward. Selection of high-potentials from among the ranks of longtime employees will be critical, as will giving all longtime employees an opportunity to participate. Some have given their best years and their best performance and will continue to do so until retirement; but, their current best may not be what the marketplace demands today.

*Best* no longer means great attendance, long tenure, or doing the job at hand. Today, *best* means listening to the customers (including internal customers) and finding creative ways to meet their needs. It also means knowing where competitors are going and beating them to the destination by implementing strategies to cut costs and increase revenues. It means referring talented potential hires, and it means bringing in a new vendor, new customer, or other resource. *Best* means suggesting ways to be faster, better, and more creative. It takes managing with five truths to get the best performance from longtime employees.

## Truth 1: We Get What We Expect

There are no "young people's jobs"—just ask Mick Jagger, Barbara Walters, Stephen Hawking, or Donald Trump. It is a myth that employees over age 40 are too old to be trained, to learn, to be flexible, or to contribute to the organization's future success. Further, it is a myth that near-retirement employees no longer desire change, career growth, learning, or achievement. Learning is a lifelong need. Consider the research:

- According to a Center for Creative Leadership study, no differences emerge by generation, gender, race, or national origin in the importance of on-the-job learning.[4] Employees of all ages want continuous learning and they prefer on-the-job training (OJT) and one-to-one coaching and feedback rather than online or computer-based learning. This bodes well for formal and informal mentoring and continuous development.

- In an Accenture study of five hundred near-retirement employees,[5]

  - 88 percent said they are willing to acquire new skills.

  - 41 percent said their company is doing a fair or poor job of providing the training needed to meet the skills challenges they face before retirement.

  - 39 percent said they are willing to work long hours.

  - 46 percent said they are willing to relocate.

  - 58 percent said they do not plan to change their retirement date. Of those planning to change their date, 74 percent plan to work longer.

  - 70 percent plan to retire from their current organization; 49 percent expect to remain in their current position until they retire. Significantly, 51 percent desire a job change before they retire!

What do the jobs at your organization require? Are the competencies of star performers detailed in job descriptions? Are the expected outputs, deadlines, and customers (external and internal) identified? If not, how can anything but average performance be expected? If global consulting firm McKinsey & Company is right in its "Value of Better Talent, 2000" research—reported in *The War for Talent*—that star performers outperform average performers by 50 to 100 percent, then both managers and employees need to understand a star performer's behaviors and outputs.[6]

Age is a positive element of an organization's diversity strategy, but it is rarely a stated element. What specific actions is your organization taking to retain the 30 percent of near-retirement employees who plan to leave and the 51 percent of near-retirement employees who want a job change? Few companies have specific plans to not only retain but reengage longtime employees. Combating discrimination has been at the forefront of the business agenda for many years, but age discrimination has taken a backseat to discrimination based on race, religion, national origin, gender, or sexual orientation. Nonetheless, all discrimination wastes employee contributions.

The business case for capitalizing on available diverse top talent has been eloquently stated many times. View the financial status of the Diversity 50 (companies cited for their outstanding diversity policies and practices) at www.DiversityInc.com. Charted against the S&P 500, NASDAQ, and Dow Jones Industrial Average companies, the combined financial results for the fifty spotlighted companies fare better. Diverse organizations are among the most profitable organizations. Further, diverse organizations have more engaged employees. A Gallup poll co-sponsored by Kaiser Permanente, the Society for Human Resource Management (SHRM), and United Parcel Service (UPS) found that employees who work for a company with highly ranked diversity efforts are more likely to stay with the company and to refer their company to others than are employees who gave their company low marks on diversity.[7]

How extensive is bias against older employees? It is so pervasive that it lurks in the hearts and minds of the longtime employees themselves. In the journal *Social Cognition,* psychologists report that men and women in their late 40s and early 50s underperformed on a standard memory test when told that they were part of a study including people over age 70.[8] "Negative images of aging on TV, in other media and in jokes reinforce negative stereotypes that can affect performance" even before people reach retirement age, according to Becca Levy, an associate professor of epidemiology and psychology at Yale University School of Public Health.[9]

Self-undermining has been well documented as a negative effect in all stereotyped groups.[10] For example, studies show that women perform less well on math exams after reading that men perform better than women. White men perform less well when they compete in math against Asian students, if they have been told that Asians outperform whites in math.

### Paying Attention and Raising Expectations Pays Dividends

Three phenomena affect performance among an organization's long-time employees.

**The Hawthorne effect:** An increase in worker productivity inspired by the psychological stimulus of being singled out and made to feel important. This finding came out of a research project (1927–1932) at the Hawthorne Plant of the Western Electric Company in Cicero, Illinois, led by Harvard Business School professor Elton Mayo, with associates F. J. Roethlisberger and William J. Dickson. Four general conclusions were drawn from the Hawthorne studies.

- **The aptitudes of individuals are imperfect predictors of job performance.** The Hawthorne researchers determined that although aptitudes give some indication of individual physical and mental potential, the amount of work people actually produce is strongly influenced by social factors.

- **Informal organization affects productivity.** The Hawthorne researchers discovered a group life among the workers. The studies also showed that the relations supervisors develop with workers tend to influence the manner in which the workers carry out directives.

- **Work-group norms affect productivity.** The Hawthorne researchers confirmed earlier studies that work groups tend to arrive at norms of what is a fair day's work.

- **The workplace is a social system.** The Hawthorne researchers came to view the workplace as a social system made up of interdependent parts.[11]

**The Pygmalion effect:** The supervisor's expectations are a key factor in how well people perform at work. In his article "Pygmalion in Management," J. Sterling Livingston noted that the Pygmalion effect enables staff to excel in response to the manager's message that they are capable of success and expected to succeed. The Pygmalion effect can also undermine staff performance when the subtle communication from the manager tells them the opposite. The Pygmalion effect, also called the power of expectations, can be summarized as:

- All supervisors have expectations of the people who report to them.

- Supervisors communicate these expectations either consciously or unconsciously.

- People pick up, consciously or unconsciously, on the expectations of their supervisors.

- People perform in ways that are consistent with the expectations they have picked up on from the supervisors.[12]

**The Galatea effect:** An individual's self-expectations can be an even more powerful element in performance than the supervisor's expectations. Employees who think they can succeed are likely to succeed. Together, aligned expectations form a powerful performance tool. The expectations of others combined with self-expectations create a person's level of motivation. While many other factors also contribute to the level of an employee's performance—including company culture, personal life experiences, education, family support, and relationships with co-workers—positive self-expectations provide the basis for consistent positive performance.[13]

---

### Engagement = Performance = Profits at Toyota

"Toyota wants people who are creative and clever about coming up with ideas and interested in making an impact," according to University of Michigan industrial and operational engineer Jeffrey Liker, author of *The Toyota Way* (2003).[14]

When an organization truly expects innovation from every employee, its processes enable people to innovate. Toyota is structured to remove bureaucracy and implement ideas quickly. Toyota has one group leader for every four team leaders. Each team leader works alongside five to six line workers. If a line worker has an efficiency idea, the team leader can get the plant's Kaizen shop to take action and put the idea into operation immediately without going through layers of approvals.[15]

Bias decreases productivity because it takes up mind-share for all parties involved. Organizations can no longer afford to have lower expectations for longtime employees—especially since both the organizations and subsequently the employees themselves begin to expect less of employees as young as age 40. Employees of any age will work up, or down, to the expectations of their supervisors, their organizations, and themselves.

A Web-based assessment developed by a Harvard-led research team found significant implicit bias among those tested. Using the Implicit Association Test (IAT), researchers found that the highest levels of bias were directed at blacks, the elderly, the disabled, the overweight, and other commonly stigmatized groups. Furthermore, the researchers found that they themselves were biased.

Researcher Tony Greenwald, a University of Washington psychology professor, was one of the first to take the test—and was immediately struck by the results. "We were initially surprised to find these biases in ourselves," says Greenwald. "After finding them in ourselves, we were not so surprised to find them in others."[16]

Employers can reduce problems with age discrimination by using uniform job interview questions for all employees and avoiding questions about age. Using uniform questions can protect employers from unconscious age bias and demonstrate a commitment to equal employment opportunity. This also applies to assessing internal candidates after hiring. Employers must remove considerations of age from their decision-making processes about promotions, training, setting expectations, and measuring results. Anything less than equal consideration of all employees is not only illegal and immoral, it is also financially foolish. The employers who win the war for talent will be those who do not allow biases to affect hiring or promotions, who expect the best from every employee, and help them achieve their best.

## Truth 2: We Get What We Reward

In a global—or even a local—marketplace, customer service is the one true differentiator. If employees are the organization's most important asset for exceeding customer expectations, surely it is the employees' ideas, daily behaviors, attention to quality and speed, and results that matter. In your organization, providing excellent customer service and any other activities that enhance individual and organizational ability to deliver excellent customer service should be the main means for employees to earn bonuses, awards, and recognition.

In our organizations, we must continuously review what we reward to ensure that employees are focused on the customers' changing needs and the marketplace's changing direction. Outstanding attendance is not equivalent to outstanding performance, though the focus on attendance in many organizations wildly overshadows the focus on performance, much less on innovation. Attendance and longevity with the organization are often greeted with awards, rewards, and parties—while no fuss is made over those employees who outperform their co-workers, finish early and help others, or get needed training to align their performance with the organization's new direction. Organizations may celebrate longevity but can no longer reward mere presence. Instead, we must reward performance.

The metrics for measuring and recognizing performance are changing. Instead of focusing exclusively on *what* work is accomplished (measuring the quantity of outputs with zero errors, or tracking and rewarding only billable hours), organizations are also rewarding *how* work is

---

### Engagement = Performance = Profits at Dierbergs

Dierbergs, a third-generation, 5,000-employee supermarket chain established in 1854 outside St. Louis, Missouri, has long been known for dedication to customer service. The store's employees innovate by listening to customer needs. Employees who look ahead to meet customer needs are recognized through the "Extra Step" program. Not only does the program make employees feel valued, it reinforces teamwork and desired behaviors. As an organizational bonus, turnover has declined from 47 percent to 25 percent over the five years that the program has been in effect, and independent surveys of customers of major chains in twenty of the nation's largest cities ranked Dierbergs as the number one store for customer service.[17]

accomplished. In any environment, if there are no rewards for responding to customer requests, preparing proposals quickly, exceeding quality requirements, preventing and overcoming problems, adhering to the organization's values, developing new business, being a team player, mentoring other employees, keeping skills current, and the like, then those activities will not occur with any regularity.

Trust in the potential for rewards and recognition plays a central role in your employees' daily performance, according to Thad Green, author of *Motivation Management* (2000). Too often, managers "consistently give employees what they deserve for poor performance, but do nothing when performance is good. This creates a trust problem."[18] Green's application model, the Belief System of Motivation and Performance, explains how employees determine how hard they will work and how well they will perform. Their effort leads to performance, which leads to outcomes, which result in satisfaction.

Trust, confidence, and satisfaction are critical in attaining desired employee performance outcomes:

- **Trust.** Assuming employees have confidence, they ask, "Will rewards be tied to my performance?" Employees must trust that rewards will be provided as promised and as their performance merits. Employees sense when their manager will not follow through—and when there will be no consequences for their performance one way or another. If employees do not trust that rewards are tied to performance, then their motivation and performance are diminished.

- **Confidence.** Given a project or task, the employee asks, "Can I do it?" Your employees must believe that the effort they are capable of giving will be sufficient to perform as requested. What do your employees believe?

- **Satisfaction.** Traditionally, managers have believed that offering satisfying outcomes or rewards will produce motivation—but what is satisfying to one person may not be to another. Employees may have confidence, and they may trust that the reward or outcome will be tied to performance, but if the reward is not satisfying, performance will likely fall short. Often tangible rewards are not the desired outcome;

coaching, time off, praise, recognition, and fair treatment may be. Avoid this issue by asking your employees what rewards would be satisfying.

Lack of appreciation—of intangible and tangible rewards—is a failure by managers to value what employees value. If one of the core components of business success is your employees' willingness to do more than a merely good job and to go above and beyond, what does your organization do to encourage higher performance?

One of the keys to ensuring performance improvement is to give prompt feedback. Feedback is an excellent source of reward and recognition. Feedback is not about filling out forms but about the relationships and conversations between managers and their staff members; it should motivate employees at all levels.

Unfortunately, many leaders treat feedback as a once-a-year event rather than an ongoing process. Annual one-hour reviews are as effective as annual one-hour diets. The only way for employees to get better at what they do is for their managers to provide candid, timely performance evaluations. In this case, timely means weekly or even daily.

"In today's environment, you have to evaluate what's changing and what's staying the same, what's working and what's no longer working," says Bruce Tulgan, author of *FAST Feedback* (1999) ("FAST" stands for "frequent, accurate, specific, timely") and founder of Rainmaker Thinking, a consulting firm based in New Haven, Connecticut. Tulgan interviewed hundreds of managers and employees for his book and documented time lag as an issue. "The once- or twice-a-year evaluation is a creature from the workplace of the past. Today's business leaders expect workers to be project-driven, results-oriented. That doesn't fit with the old model of reviewing performance every 6 or 12 months," he says.[19]

Yearly or twice-yearly goal setting and individual development plans are critical elements for aligning employee performance with departmental and individual goals, but they do not motivate, change behaviors, or improve performance by themselves. Regular documented goal setting and performance reviews fulfill legal needs, but prompt feedback keeps positive performance coming and corrects underperformance early. A just-in-time workforce requires just-in-time feedback. Managers can build timely feedback into routine meetings and memos, or they can deliver feedback through e-mail, voice mail, or short notes. Ideally, managers should give employees daily feedback—but both content and timing are important. Remember, praise in public and criticize in private. Also, avoid giving important feedback on the fly. Once the majority of your managers begin practicing Tulgan's "FAST Feedback," this behavior change will create a dynamic environment of ongoing results-oriented dialogue, build trust, increase productivity, cut turnaround time, and invigorate your corporate culture.

In Chapter 1, I discussed truly loyal employees and cited their willingness to participate in 360-degree feedback, career planning, training classes, mentor programs, job description upgrades, and promotions. What about trapped employees who have terrific attendance records and meet their minimum goals but do not raise their hand for one extra assignment? One reason may be a lack of rewards.

If you have a higher percentage of truly loyal employees (who will participate in the activities that move the organization forward, see themselves with the company for the next two years, and will decline offers) than does your competition, you have a genuine edge. While the Walker study shows that 86 percent of executives in upper management

---

### Engagement = Performance = Profits at Glenroy

At Glenroy, a Wisconsin manufacturer, employee engagement is very high. The company literally burned its employee manuals, and has turned to its employees for input in many areas including its approach to pay. Several weeks after the bonfire, it was time for annual performance appraisals and salary reviews. Management was clear: reviews were on the ash heap of history. Glenroy management needed to determine what kinds of raises employees would get. The improved approach? Employee peer groups decided on their own raises.

Glenroy divided its workforce into groups based on job classification. It was up to those peer groups to set their raises. In most cases, executive vice president Michael Dean reports, the peer groups were tougher than management would have been. The company later had to adjust many of the raises upward. "We treat people like adults," says Dean. "That's the essence of leadership."[20]

are truly loyal, only 33 percent of supervisors and 28 percent of individual contributors are in the truly loyal category.[21] Could it be that supervisors who are not rewarded with something of value in turn withhold rewards from their staff?

In the same study, 41 percent of employees with ten to nineteen years of tenure describe themselves as trapped (would leave if they could) and 24 percent as high risk (actively looking for a new job); employees with twenty years or more of service are slightly more loyal, with only 31 percent describing themselves as trapped but 25 percent actively searching for a job.

What could productivity be like if the majority of your second-decade employees did not feel trapped or were not conducting job searches? What if those employees felt truly loyal?

Celebrate longevity but *reward* performance and loyalty. Reward the best from every employee. Table 3 lists the industries with the highest percentage of truly loyal employees.[22] If your industry overall does not have a high level of employee loyalty, review what is rewarded. With changes to the reward and recognition processes, your organization can defy the statistics.

| TABLE 3 THE LOYALTY LEADERS | | |
|---|---|---|
| RANKING | INDUSTRY | PERCENTAGE OF TRULY LOYAL EMPLOYEES |
| 1 | Nonprofit | 39 |
| 2 | Health Care | 39 |
| 3 | Hospital | 38 |
| 4 | IT | 36 |
| 5 | Financial Services | 33 |
| 6 | Retail Trade | 32 |
| 7 | Manufacturing | 31 |
| 8 | Government | 27 |

## Truth 3: We Get What We Encourage

No matter your services or products, innovation is the key to sustainable future profits. The makers of buggy whips didn't believe it in 1900. The makers of watches didn't believe it in 2000. Believe it.

By the end of 2004, as the reality of a global marketplace was sinking in, 78 percent of CEOs surveyed by the Conference Board said that stimulating innovation and building creativity are top priorities for their company.[23] The ability to innovate based on newly acquired knowledge is the key to keeping companies competitive.

In this age of commoditization, innovation is the only currency of competition. If, as some believe, the best ideas come from outside the organization, then how does a company like Nokia account for the continuous development of dozens of cell phones with new features every year? How does the creative team inside Cirque du Soleil continue to develop dazzling new shows?

---

### Engagement = Performance = Profits at Wal-Mart

"Always Low Prices—Always" is not possible at Wal-Mart without ongoing employee innovation and creativity. In 2005, after Katrina and Rita became household names and prices at the gas pump were anything but low, Lee Scott, Wal-Mart's CEO, challenged his staff to "lower the price of living and make a difference for our customers." An employee's innovative idea to help customers save money on utility bills by changing from incandescent lightbulbs to compact fluorescent lights (CFLs) has also saved Wal-Mart money on its electric bills and created new jobs at GE.

One CFL equals six to ten incandescent lightbulbs because it will last five to ten years. As a bonus, CFLs use 70 to 80 percent less energy. By replacing incandescent lightbulbs with compact fluorescent lights (CFLs) in its 3,230 stores, Wal-Mart saves $6 million a year.

In addition to using CFLs in its stores, Wal-Mart plans to sell 100 million CFLs annually; it has partnered with GE to make this target reachable by manufacturing enough energy smart bulbs. By the end of 2005, thanks in part to this alliance, GE had tripled its CFL manufacturing capacity.[24]

---

Innovation and creativity cannot be commanded, but both can be encouraged. In organizations with an innovation culture, creativity can be the expected outcome, not a surprise. Unfortunately, all it takes to extinguish the first flicker of new ideas is a manager who says, "When I want your ideas, I'll ask for them." Alternatively, amazing creativity flourishes when a manager does ask for ideas!

To innovate, every employee needs to understand industry issues and changing customer needs and to have access to a variety of learning tools. Confidence in their ability to innovate is the fuel for thought that all employees need from management. Too many organizations have narrowly defined and relied on a small number of "creative types"—in some cases, one person—to provide all product development ideas. Innovation must come not only in products, however, but in processes, procedures, and interactions with customers, referral sources for business, and new hires—every aspect of the business. Every department and every function needs the benefit of innovation to survive and thrive. Only when there are few or no barriers to employee performance and customer service will costs be lower and profits higher.

Creating a culture of innovation is an ambitious but ever more necessary strategy. It cannot be accomplished without the active participation of longtime employees. It is so necessary that companies as different as Google, Cargill, Clorox, and Apple Computer have innovation champions.[25]

Every organization can develop a culture of innovation, but it starts with giving all employees—even Boomers and Veterans—positive hands-on management. Managing for innovation and creativity requires addressing four employee needs:

- The need to be recognized as a source of unique potential and talents. Management must believe that employees can do whatever needs to be done.

- The need to trust and be trusted. Management must allow employees to make decisions—and even mistakes.

---

### Engagement = Performance = Profits at Google

Marissa Mayer, vice president of search products and user experience for Google, is a big reason why Google functions as an open social network where every piece of work is available to every employee on the company's intranet. This enables employees to join projects, find relevant expertise, or consult internally among those working on similar projects. Innovators are engaged at Google. Openness is balanced with a rigid, procedure-filled, structure for reviewing new features for the Web site. Presentations are held to ten minutes as the review team adds, deletes, and changes features while a giant clock counts down. Innovation at lightning speed is a daily occurrence. At Google, some "Notions of Innovations" include

- Expect ideas to come from everywhere. Expect every employee to innovate, even the Finance team.

- Share everything you can. Every idea, every project, every deadline is accessible on the intranet.[26]

- Use your license to dream. Employees get a free day a week—and 50 percent of new product launches come from this "20 percent" time.

- Aim for innovation, not instant perfection. Google beta tests early and often before releasing new features.

- Don't kill projects—morph them. There is always a kernel that can be salvaged.

---

- The need to be engaged with their work, their peers, their customers, and the larger community. Management must anoint each employee as a company ambassador.

- The need to remain competitive through continuous learning. Management must give employees the industry knowledge and skills to be responsive to changing customer and market needs.

## Truth 4: We Get What We Enable

Employee engagement is a response to daily work life. Every employee wakes up every day and decides whether to "git 'er done" with or without discretionary effort.

Employees who are learning are not coasting. Organizations enable employee engagement through a variety of programs and experiences. Traditional employee development must be expanded beyond its narrow focus on hard skills—and even beyond the development of specific soft skills. Employee development needs to include the expectation of and the tools for innovation.

- **Training in decision making, working in cross-functional teams, basic project management, and customer focus.** These four skills are fundamental today in every function, whether the employee has a job facing the public or not. No longer can employees work without consideration for others (peers or customers), passively doing only the tasks they are actually assigned. Lack of these four skills hinders employees' ability to deliver quality and efficiency, much less creativity and innovation. Courses are often available through the local Chamber of Commerce, adult education programs, or a local chapter of the American Society for Training and Development (ASTD).

- **Training in facilitation and consensus building.** As part of empowering decision making, every longtime employee should be able to run and contribute to a brainstorming meeting that gets results. Too many employees have been exposed to poorly run meetings where ideas are shot down immediately ("We've already tried that," "You're too old [or young], too set in your ways [or inexperienced], or too different [in sex, race, ethnicity] to understand the problem [or to have a good solution]").

  Great facilitators know how to ask questions, draw out participants, give and receive feedback, handle hecklers, and gather ideas so that the ideas themselves can be critiqued, not the participants. As a tool to develop longtime employees—or any employees—quickly, consider starting a chapter of Toastmasters (http://www.toastmasters. org/about.asp) at your company. Participants will quickly learn to deliver great presentations, confidently lead teams and conduct meetings, give and receive constructive evaluations, and become better listeners. Specific classes in consensus building are available through local ASTD chapters.

- **Job shadowing and job swapping: employees on loan to different departments, customers, or vendors.** To expand employees' internal horizons, nothing has a better effect than spending a day "walking in someone else's shoes." Whether observing or participating, this tool can open the participants' eyes to the challenges of another position, spark their imagination to solve interdepartmental issues, and potentially be the catalyst for pursuing a position with the host department.

- **Mentoring up, down, peer-to-peer, inside and outside the organization.** Many organizations talk about mentoring but far fewer actually use it as a development and retention tool. The irony is that all parties benefit from the experience, and employees with more than one mentor benefit the most. Mentoring programs are best developed as a response to a need that is readily acknowledged within the organization, not because they are the employee development flavor of the month.

    Longtime employees can be mentors or protégés. The format can vary: one-to-one or one-to-many; up, down, peer-to-peer; cross-functional or cross-departmental; in person or via phone, e-mail, or Internet voice connection; and inside or outside the organization. Available mentors and protégés may post their biographies and other information on company intranet sites to facilitate the matching process. Mentoring duos who communicate regularly are more productive and satisfied than are those who communicate sporadically. Myrna Marofsky and Ann Johnson's *Getting Started with Mentoring* is a practical guide to initiating a mentoring program.[27]

- **Immersion in the communication efficiency tools of the new workplace: voice mail, e-mail, instant messaging, and text messaging.** A Pew Internet & American Life Project survey shows that as of December 2006, 71 percent of people between ages 50 and 64 and 32 percent of people age 65 and older are online daily.[28] Speed and quality of communication is the critical tool in organizations that enables responsiveness to marketplace or customer-specific changes.

Too few companies make e-mail and other communication tools—and etiquette training—available to longtime employees. Using technology is not just a job skill; it is a life skill.

Employees who function without voice mail, e-mail, and other high-tech tools cannot fail to be out of the loop in their department, company, or industry. Lack of Internet access cuts off access to e-learning and webinars (Web-based training meetings). Longtime employees need just-in-time development tools, too. Anything less guarantees slower performance.

## Truth 5: We Get What We Measure

We track too many irrelevant metrics or metrics that do not tell the complete story. Too often, we measure activity, not results. Results-oriented metrics focus on customer satisfaction, employee contributions to the organization's strategic goals via employee, vendor, or other referrals or ideas, and delivery of quality and quantity while adhering to the organization's values and branding statement. Where in your performance management system are employees held accountable for genuine responsiveness to customers and the other essentials of the modern environment? What processes or tools are available to help them meet these goals?

---

**Engagement = Performance = Profits at Your Organization**

New hires, 20-something kids (in their elders' eyes), are teaching managers and other longtime employees about using technology at organizations nationwide. Procter & Gamble, Deloitte & Touche, and the Seattle Public Schools have made formal reverse mentoring a success, while reducing training costs. "They [Gen Ys] always have a faster, better way of getting information," says Alicia Blain, vice president for information systems at Visa International in Miami.

For some longtime employees, going outside their organization by tapping their local Chamber of Commerce or professional organization might make it easier on their ego to ask for help learning something specific about technology.[29]

---

Develop relevant metrics with input from your employees. When well done, individual performance management is a tool that can help build the relationship between employee and supervisor and between both and the larger organization. Performance management systems should recognize excellence, build on strengths, and provide development plans to build new skills or correct deficiencies.

Share the overall strategy of the organization with all employees, as well as the need for excellent individual performance in a competitive marketplace. In one-to-one meetings with employees, managers should be sure that individual performance expectations are tied to the strategy, and reiterate that employees should not expect an annual merit increase unless specific goals are met. Put it in writing and ask employees to sign a document stating that they understand their goals for the year.

Create many opportunities for employees at all levels to contribute ideas and enhancements to their own job and to the overall operations of the department or organization. Create a process that ensures that their ideas will be reviewed and given serious consideration. Ask employees how they can support the achievement of strategic goals—and hold them accountable for following through.

## IT'S TIME FOR COORDINATED ACTION

Myth busting is a daily activity for employers of choice, those organizations determined to be the career destination of innovative, creative top talent. To position your organization as an employer of choice for all generations whose employees are energized, productive, and innovative every day, the five engagement truths must become operational. What does your organization expect, reward, encourage, enable, and measure? Every organization is perfectly designed to deliver the results that it gets—from longtime (and all) employees. Don't like your organization's current results? Become a myth-buster!

## Leverage Longtime Employees

- **For all managers:** How is bias preventing full engagement in your organization? Tackle hidden bias with the Implicit Association Test. Go to https://implicit.harvard.edu/implicit/ and take the test. Anonymity and security of individual responses are ensured.

- **For HR:** How can you reverse bias and ignite performance? Provide all managers and employees with inclusion training. If your organization does not have inclusion training, contact your local Diversity Roundtable or go to www.DiversityInc.com for resources.

- **For senior management:** How can you measure the contributions of longtime employees? Create a "Diversity Dashboard" or scorecard to track a range of diversity metrics. Develop metrics for the training, lateral career moves, and promotion rates of longtime employees, training participation, career path movement, rehiring, compensation rates, and other relevant indicators of fairness.

- **For senior management and HR:** Is your performance management system for all employees designed to ensure customer responsiveness and operating according to the values of the organization? If the only parameters are "on time and on budget," that is all employees will deliver.

• • • •

CHAPTER

# 5

# • • • • Capture Knowledge, Develop Competencies

The economic resilience of the United States is based on our long-term ability to attract, engage, and retain top talent both locally and globally. Today, that means attracting, engaging, and retaining top talent among current and even past employees—not just future employees. Your organization's competitive advantage comes down to how well you and your managers develop employees' skills and tap into knowledge and abilities already embodied in your workforce. That is why losing your Boomers and Veterans to early and on-time retirement is going to have such an impact.

Smart organizations are looking to strategic workforce planning to analyze and forecast the talent that will be needed to execute their business strategy. This is not a count of how many jobs or people are needed: it is a close look at the skills, knowledge, and abilities needed at specific times to meet specific needs. It requires an understanding of the organization's strategic business plan, the implications for the company's workforce, and the availability of internal and external talent to fill gaps. It requires being ready to train, but not relying on training alone. Top talent in almost any position is identified not so much by hard skills as by soft skills, decision-making ability, relationships, project experiences, and deep customer, product, and industry knowledge.

Hard skills are easily taught in a finite period; increasing knowledge requires multiple experiences. Instead of looking outside the organization for new blood, take a look inside. Many of the best candidates to take your organization into an innovative, profitable future are on staff right now—or were on someone's staff not long ago.

The key advantage to mining longtime employees as a resource begins with the observation that the United States currently has more than 24.6 million workers age 55 or older, more than at any other point in our history.[1] But these workers have more than numbers going for them; their real advantage is their deep knowledge of customers and products, their core competencies, and their general workplace professionalism. Aerospace, health care, utilities, energy, oil, and government sectors are expected to be the hardest hit by the massive Baby Boomer retirement, which will decrease the U.S. workforce by as much as 40 percent.[2]

Today, managers regret one in five new hires.[3] Newer hires often have the latest technology skills, but, according to comments from human resources professionals in the "2005 Future of the U.S. Labor Pool" study, lack such competencies as business knowledge; verbal, analytical, and writing skills; and overall professionalism.[4]

Building these competencies in newer employees is a critical need, but, in the meantime, organizations cannot afford the customer and product knowledge loss they suffer every time a longtime employee retires. While most organizations are working feverishly to train their newer hires, they must simultaneously inspire and motivate longtime employees to strengthen their customer relationships, document their knowledge, mentor their Gen X and Gen Y colleagues in order to build bench strength—and delay retirement. None of these needed activities is currently in longtime employees' job descriptions.

By 2010, 20 percent of the workforce will be over age 55.[5] Delaying employee retirements by five years, from age 62 to age 67, would raise the labor supply by 4.4 percent, according to the Urban Institute.[6] Organizations—and Social Security—need every competitive strategy they can muster. Healthy, working older employees could make a significant difference to the bottom line at your organization—and would add to the solvency of Social Security, too, since FICA tax revenues would grow and there would be fewer retirees to support.

While disengagement can cause longtime employees to retire on the job and stay, they will retire early or on time—and take their knowledge with them—even if they're engaged, if they find themselves needing but not getting support from their employer for child care or elder care, returning to school, or dealing with personal health issues.

Just as disengagement can be anticipated and minimized, so can early retirement and even on-time retirement. This chapter focuses on organizational responses that can delay retirement, capture needed knowledge, and create long-term pre- and post-retirement relationships that are win-win for the organization and the employee.

## WHERE'S THE FIRE?

Continuous abundant labor has been taken for granted like drinkable water or clean air. Your organization cannot grow without talented workers. Either you hire new talented employees and accelerate their learning curve dramatically, or you energize the performance of the talented employees you have on staff. Today, the unemployment rate is below 5 percent. In some locales, it is below 3 percent. While the overall slower growth rate of the labor force is noticeable now at 1.2 percent, here's the fire: the growth rate will slow to .06 percent for 2010 to 2015, and it will be just .02 percent for 2015 to 2025. Worse, growth in the population of well-educated, tech-savvy, top-quality labor may grind to a halt. When Baby Boomers entered the workforce, they were better educated than the workers they replaced. Today, new workers are at best at the same education level as retiring workers; and immigrants are more likely to be less educated than average American-born employees, but very focused on raising the education level of their children.[7] We need to welcome hardworking immigrants for their current and future contributions, hire the best candidates, and also keep our educated, knowledgeable longtime workers on staff as long as possible.

# ANTICIPATE AND MINIMIZE
# EARLY RETIREMENT

The decision to stay with an employer is a rational one (I get a paycheck and benefits, I know my job, My commute is short), but the decision to perform above and beyond is emotional (I love the people here—especially my boss, I don't want to let down my team, My work is so interesting, I want to leave a legacy). Employers want to delay the retirement of engaged employees who are near retirement but still have the willingness to try new things and share their knowledge. The difficulty is that most employers have no idea how many of their employees are going to retire in the next five years, how many are eligible for early retirement, when their employees plan to retire, or which functions will be most affected.

In an Accenture study,[8] 58 percent of survey respondents said they do not plan to change their retirement date, while 41 percent said they have made a change. Of those planning to change their date, 74 percent said they plan to work longer. This means that if a hundred employees are near retirement, fifty-eight of them plan to stay only as long as scheduled, while thirty-two want to extend their stay. The challenge is to significantly increase that last figure.

Never assume that "good ol' Sal" would never want a different job. In fact, she just might! In the same study, 70 percent of near-retirement employees plan to stay with their current organization until they retire—which means 30 percent plan to leave—and 49 percent expect to remain in their current position until they retire—which means 51 percent would like new challenges, new titles, and new positions! If leaving is the only way to stay challenged, many of your most capable longtime employees will leave!

Organizations have a long history of policies and benefits aimed at employees during their child-rearing years. Organizational wisdom has been that Gen X and Gen Y employees work to live and older employees live to work. The assumption is that few, if any, longtime employees have personal issues or desires that conflict with organizational goals and that they will remain with their company even if their work needs go unmet. In a world of job choice, however, even longtime employees will leave to seek new challenges, better benefits, and more flexible work arrangements. Further, you can expect them to succeed in getting hired away since their productivity makes them cost-effective employees.

Personal and work lives are blending due to technology and the need to operate 24/7, yet the availability of qualified employees to work standard eight- or twelve-hour shifts is dwindling rapidly. To provide the best customer service will require many different work arrangements used simultaneously. Expect Boomers and Veterans as well as younger employees to seek resources and alternatives to assist with

- **Child care.** Record numbers of men and women over age 50 are welcoming babies into their lives through pregnancy, adoption, and surrogacy. Some are also taking on the care of grandchildren or other relatives. Vouchers and programs for child care and after-school care need to be extended to any dependent child.

- **Elder care.** Whether for parents, in-laws, or siblings, at least 25 percent of employees need resources for long-distance care management, adult day care, respite care, hospice, and other services. A compilation of care providers could easily be made available on your organization's intranet. A support group of employees with elder care issues could help employees stay focused on their job responsibilities by multiplying their resources.

- **Returning to school.** Second and third careers are becoming more common. Tuition reimbursement for employees of any age—with any career goal—will keep them engaged and on staff at least until graduation. Tuition costs less than turnover or early retirement, and it can be used to create a new source of future hires from among experienced employees. Tuition reimbursement and scholarships for children or grandchildren are also enticing benefits. Accommodation of class schedules is becoming a common policy in organizations of all sizes. If your longtime employees' new skills and knowledge can be used in-house, it would be ideal. If their new skills and knowledge can be used by a vendor or customer, great! They will become alumni of your organization and remain friends.

- **Health issues.** There is a general perception that workers in the 50-plus age group cost more to employ than younger workers. However, any additional costs are minimal when measured against the higher productivity and lower absenteeism of these longtime workers. Studies found that employees age 50 to 65 use on average 1.4 to 2.2 times as much health care as workers in their 30s and 40s. Yet the overall health of individuals near or past typical retirement age is much improved compared to past decades. The rate of chronic disability among those over 65 has plunged to below 20 percent.[9] According to a 2002 survey on employer incentives to hire people with disabilities, 38 percent of employers spent nothing on reasonable accommodations, 28 percent spent $1,000 or less, 8 percent spent between $1,000 and $5,000, and 14 percent spent more than $5,000.[10] With minimal action and cost, difficulties posed by many disabilities can be minimized or avoided. Still, health can be a factor in an employee's decision to cut back hours or to retire early.

## WELLNESS IS THE WAY

Could 55 be the new 35? Why not! Staying mentally and physically in shape is not only possible at any age, it can be done easily and in many ways. Employees need to pursue new physical and mental skills, and then hone them to maintain a higher level of innovation capability.

Your future will likely be longer than you think—and the same is true for your employees. Long-term care provider Genworth Financial unveiled an advertising campaign featuring remarkably vital centenarians.[11] Frank Shearer, a motivational speaker, celebrated his 100th birthday by water skiing in Acapulco. Helen Green, at 104, is still an engaging public speaker. She sent the first of many regular e-mail messages at age 95.

If Frank and Helen can stay fit and learn new skills, your employees can too. Unless water skiing can improve your bottom line, however, focus on developing more relevant skills.

The truth is, we love our cars more than we love ourselves. Preventive maintenance such as checking tire pressure, replacing wiper blades, and listening weekly to NPR's *Car Talk* are routine care for our precious automobiles. Yet we scrimp on taking even the smallest steps to keep our body healthy and our mind sharp. It shows in the mirror and in our health care premiums. What if you could change what you see in the mirror and minimize health care insurance costs while increasing creativity, capturing knowledge, and building both a library and a living storehouse of industry, product, and customer knowledge? It can be done! It must be done.

Physical and mental acuity are vital in life and at work. To keep and develop both, an ounce of prevention is worth more than a pound of cure because the cost of a cure is so high. The cost is evident in health care premiums; but costs also show up in higher *presenteeism* (working when ill—which causes others to become ill), lower productivity, and early retirements.

In many instances, employers are adopting programs that promote healthy behaviors in an effort to minimize the cost of health care premiums. Focusing on specific health risks such as smoking or obesity has shifted the way employers are addressing the costs related to health care. The payoff is that healthy older workers are highly productive, highly engaged, and motivated to exceed expectations on the job.[12]

If we are going to beat our competition because we are staffed with innovative, productive, engaged up-and-comers in the post-40 age group, wellness programs must become foundation elements, especially in organizations with deep knowledge to capture and pass on. We need employees with healthy bodies and minds who can focus on their customers' needs and on generating innovative solutions.

Towers Perrin's research suggests building a "culture of health" by focusing on the underlying causes of health care cost increases (instead of just looking at the costs alone) and taking a systematic approach to identifying and acting on opportunities for improvement.[13] Organizations need to design, execute, and communicate programs that encourage employees to adopt and maintain healthy lifestyles, engage vendors and providers to deliver efficient solutions, and encourage the organization's leaders to model and reward healthy behaviors.

Wellness programs are approached differently in different organizations depending on what is driving health care costs. An analysis is worth the effort. Wellness programs could involve any of the following measures:

- Gun safety, CPR training, and the basics of first aid if hunting season accidents are a cost factor

- Pedometers and competitions to rack up 10,000 steps or more a day if your employees would otherwise "drive their desks" and send e-mail instead of walking down the hall

- Stress management classes, nutrition education, healthy take-home dinners, vending machines stocked with apples and high-fiber energy bars, and on-site health checks to keep employees focused on healthy habits

- Aerobics classes on-site, gym memberships, and personal coaches if employees are overweight and/or have high rates of diabetes, heart disease, and other health issues

Research shows that those organizations that have invested in a greater number of health and productivity best practices (twenty or more practices) are more likely to achieve desired outcomes than are those organizations with lower investments (ten or fewer practices).[14] As a result of focusing intensely on putting more health and productivity best practices in place, companies have reduced lost time, improved employee understanding of health improvement, increased employee satisfaction with benefits, improved overall employee health, and reduced turnover.

A Watson Wyatt study, "Staying @ Work," puts a spotlight on those practices associated with better rates and shorter duration of absence and short-term disability.[15] Desired specific outcomes can be seen following implementation practices aimed at the following:

1. Lower incidental absence rates
   - Improving employee work–life balance
   - Newsletter articles

- Online health and prevention education information
- Preventive care reminders
- Self-care guides

2. Shorter incidental absence duration
   - Improving employee work–life balance
   - Integrated health and disability data
   - Self-care guides

3. Lower short-term disability (STD) rates
   - Health risk appraisals and screenings
   - Integrated health and disability data
   - Newsletter articles
   - Preventive care reminders

4. Shorter short-term disability (STD) duration
   - Health promotion programs
   - Health risk appraisals and screenings
   - Improving employee work–life balance
   - Integrated health and disability data
   - On-site medical clinics
   - Preventive care reminders
   - Supervisor involvement in absence management programs

Organizations with the lowest health care costs, according to Towers Perrin, focus on health as a top priority, gear their programs to prevent and manage illness, educate employees to do the right things, hold employees accountable, and manage vendors aggressively.[16]

Wellness is not just for bodies—it is for minds, too. Aerobics, according to a recent study by the University of Illinois, Urbana, has significant brain benefits.[17] "The people who exercised had the brain volumes of people three years younger," according to professor Arthur Kramer. As reported in the November 2006 issue of the *Journal of Gerontology: Medical Sciences,* after three months of aerobics, elderly people who participated as little as three hours a week increased the brain's volume of gray matter (actual neurons) and white matter (connections between neurons) and, as a result, experienced greater ease switching between mental tasks and greater ability to screen out distractions.

We know that employees will work up to (or down to) the expectations of their manager and organization. It stands to reason that meeting high expectations is easiest when mental muscles are exercised regularly, too.

In *Keep Your Brain Alive,* Lawrence Katz, an investigator with Duke University's Howard Hughes Medical Institution, says that new challenges stimulate mental sharpness.[18] You can improve brain function by doing the same things differently. He calls this activity "neurobic exercises." Simple actions keep the mind fresh:

- Drive home following a new route tonight. Drive home yet a different way tomorrow evening.

- Learn a new skill. Use it. Use it again tomorrow.

- Take a brisk ten-minute walk for your next break. Walk a different route tomorrow.

- If crossword puzzles are easy for you, try Sudoku. And vice versa.

- Learn five useful words in a foreign language valuable to your specific workplace. Use them. Next week, learn five more words. Use all ten words that week, and keep this up week after week.

- Listen to Mozart for ten minutes. Tomorrow, listen to Bach.

- Try writing or brushing your teeth with the other hand. Then try to do it with both hands at the same time using two toothbrushes.

Challenge yourself—and your employees—to fight off the effects of mental aging. It can take as little as three hours of aerobic exercise—and some neurobic exercise—a week. We spend that much time on our cars, pets, and hair. Remember, we get what we expect!

## CAPTURE KNOWLEDGE

Much has been written but little actually accomplished in the area of knowledge transfer. Mentoring is much discussed as the preferred means to pass on knowledge, but mentoring programs are rarely formalized, measured, or made part of organizational culture. Not only is one-to-one transfer of knowledge laborious, rarely rewarded, and often unwelcomed by both the transmitter and the recipient, it proves worthless if the recipient leaves the organization. That is not to say that mentoring cannot be an excellent tool for knowledge transfer—it simply cannot be the only tool. With turnover rates as high as they are among Gen X and Gen Y employees in any organization, the real focus should be on knowledge capture.

There is no one best way to select, document, access, or transfer knowledge. The organizational culture, demographics, and availability of IT software will affect not only how knowledge is captured but also what knowledge is valued. As is true with any sweeping culture change, buy-in from employees is critical for knowledge capture to occur. If the culture is one that does not normally share information, people are likely to resist the idea of participating. Keeping skill and project profiles updated could become a key component of semiannual performance reviews as a way to document needed information. Hold up pay increases until it is done. Another success factor will be to keep the focus of the information gathering specific and succinct. Do not try to document everything.

The technology to capture and classify knowledge is evolving rapidly. Companies such as AskMe Corp., Tacit Knowledge Systems, and Autonomy sell expert locator systems. Ideally, the captured knowledge will be easily searchable, and a frequently checked internal bulletin board will enable employees to ask each other for information that may be buried in the system and for ways to get in touch with individuals with greater knowledge.

Approach knowledge capture strategically. A systemic approach will be more worthwhile than a person- or position-specific solution. Tie all initiatives to the organization's strategy. Note where lost knowledge could do the most harm to the performance of the organization. Determine which functions are most critical: production, sales, R&D, and so on. Ask what cultural elements, such as career development processes, job design, or retirement policies, could be changed to facilitate knowledge capture.

Knowledge capture can start as simply as having every employee document job tasks in a series of job aids. A *job aid* is a repository for information, processes, or perspectives that is external to the individual and that supports work and activity by directing, guiding, and enlightening performance.[19]

A job aid is a simple set of instructions (words or visuals) that enable a new hire or a temp to satisfactorily perform a specific task on time, with the correct frequency and desired outcome.

Building on the foundation of job aids, collect stories for case studies that demonstrate the problem-solving, prioritization, customer focus, multitasking, or other competencies that provide outstanding results. Every employee has work accomplishments and every department manager knows which three to four projects stood out in the past few years. Each case study should include answers to questions such as these:

- What was the objective of this project?

- What were the barriers to be overcome?

- How did you prepare before initiating this project? (resources assembled, team selection criteria, and so on)

- What metrics were developed and used to measure the outcome?

- What special actions or competencies enabled the success of this project?

- How did the client receive this project? How do you know?

- For others with similar projects to complete, what are the learnings or recommendations from this project?

Knowledge capture would not be complete without a database of employee (and retiree) skills and projects. If alliances outside the organization play a critical role in your organization's successes, add to the database examples of how to build and maintain those relationships, how to select allies, and similar processes. What does your organization's strategy require if it is to succeed? What it does not need is the sudden loss of its most knowledgeable staff.

---

### Knowledge Capture European Style

Two European Union research projects have been established to provide access to critical business information and to help employees and companies with skill-set management. The APOSDLE project is intended to aid employees by gathering all the knowledge capital available in the workplace. The system is aware of available resources and alerts employees to those that are relevant. Resources include databases, publications, presentations and documents, lists of courses available, access to company documents, and the insight of experienced employees.

"APOSDLE will work in the background, intuiting what information the employee needs and then providing a menu of resources," says Stefanie Lindstaedt, scientific coordinator for the APOSDLE project. "A worker might see the name of a colleague who is an expert in her area of interest. She could record an interview with the colleague, and the recording itself would become a new resource," she adds.

PROLIX is a skill-set management project that deals with the problem of fitting structured content to an employee's training necessities. "Right now most learning issues are dealt with by the HR department," says Volker Zimmerman, CEO of e-learning company IMC and coordinator of PROLIX. However, "company-based learning needs to be imbedded in business needs, so when a company changes its processes or procedures, the employee-training required to execute the changes develops in parallel," explains Zimmerman. The "PROLIX system will deliver the exact skill-set required to execute a new, optimized business process."[20]

---

## RECONSTRUCT RETIREMENT

Until now, retirement has been an all-or-nothing affair. On a day designated by the employer or the employee, people gather for a party where war stories are told and the employee is thanked for service, and then the employee heads out of the company parking lot for the last time. Remaining employees scavenge the newly vacated workspace before a new hire is brought on board. Files are shredded, file folders recycled, and file cabinets moved to other offices. Information about undocumented current and past projects, secret formulas, and the myriad contacts inside and outside the organization that enabled quick problem solving is too often lost. Study after study says that this approach is too much of a shock for both the organization and the individual, so alternatives such as phased retirement—a reduction of hours worked until the actual retirement date—are being offered.

## REDEFINE RETENTION

Retention used to mean continuous employment with the same employer. The term was used primarily in conjunction with full-time employment. Today, managers often see retention as keeping people in the same job—or certainly in the same department—for more than 3.2 years. In our project-driven, knowledge-bound workplaces, retention needs a more flexible definition and approach. The goal must not be just to keep long-time employees on board forty or more hours a week. Instead, the goal must be to keep the A players—the top talent—around to meet specific goals, satisfy customers, and keep quality levels high in whatever work configuration makes best use of the skills available and keeps the individuals engaged. Retention can be a concept used with new hires, traditional high-potentials or up-and-comers, near-retirement employees, or retirees (yours or another organization's). Today, retention can include an as-needed or even seasonal relationship with specific retirees who have special skills, knowledge, and abilities. Retain engaged workers, not just bodies or headcount. Only engaged individuals ensure excellence.

AARP (formerly called the American Association of Retired Persons) compiles an annual list of the top fifty employers for workers over 50. In surveys conducted to determine the winners, AARP found that older workers want more flexibility in their job, by implementing such tools as phased retirement, telecommuting, and job sharing.[21] The percentage of employees over 50 who want alternative work arrangements is so high that employers should expect questions addressing this topic during interviews with older candidates, such as how many older workers the company has, if there is a phased retirement system or age diversity

## Engagement = Performance = Benefits for FHN

In 2006, FHN, a regional health care system serving the needs of the people of northwest Illinois and southern Wisconsin, was named one of three Employers of the Year by the Illinois Employers' Association and one of twelve finalists in the Society for Human Resource Management's Human Capital Leadership Awards in the Competitive Workforce Award category for responding to key workforce trends and needs. One of those needs was the rethinking of retirement.

After meeting several times with 108 members of the Silver Eagles, a group of employees with more than twenty-five years of service each, FHN's senior management approved the "Phased Retirement Program," which was designed to enable near-retirement staff members to participate in the regular employee health care benefits while working fewer hours than normally required for that benefit. Those employees would be reimbursed for a portion of their COBRA premium costs as a way to extend their time on staff at FHN. To be eligible for this pilot program, an employee must meet the following criteria:

- Has applied for and is receiving FHN pension benefits

- Was classified and working full-time, flex full-time, or benefit eligible part-time at the time of phased retirement

- Achieved a minimum of 320 out of a possible 500 points on the most recent performance assessment

- Was not placed on a Work Improvement Plan or Corrective Counseling within the past year

- Was working in a direct clinical role within FHN at the time of phased retirement (this may change at the conclusion of the two-year pilot program)

- Was employed with FHN for a minimum of ten years prior to the beginning of the phased retirement program

- Is working in a position and department in which the phased work requirement can be initiated or is willing to work in an area in which the requirements can be implemented

The phased work requirement is to work a minimum of two shifts per pay period and be available to work one additional shift per pay period.

> The monetary support toward the COBRA premiums for staff who qualify for this program is based on the following formula: years of service x 2 = percent of monthly COBRA contribution by FHN. The minimum FHN contribution toward this program is 25 percent and the maximum contribution is 80 percent.[22]

training, and how much flexibility the company offers workers nearing retirement.

Alternative work arrangements are attractors for current as well as prospective employees of all ages. Organizations that keep a database of current employee and retiree résumés as well as employee and retiree skills, project experience, industry sales experience, or other specialized equipment or manufacturing experience are able to redeploy existing employees more efficiently and pull in retirees as needed for projects. Peaks and valleys of work, vacations, unexpected illnesses, and surprise customer demands need not require bringing in temporary workers unfamiliar with your business.

Alternative work arrangements are not entitlements for all employees, nor are all situations conducive to alternative work schedules. Requests must be evaluated on a case-by-case basis and must have manager approval and assistance to be successful. Approval of alternative work schedule requests should be based on whether it benefits the employee,

### Engagement = Performance = Profits at Atlantic Health

New Jersey's Atlantic Health System, number 22 on AARP's 2006 "Best Employers for Workers over 50" list, has created a flexible work option to retain their most experienced older workers. Atlantic Health employees can work up to 999 hours a year—part-time, per diem, or on special assignment projects—and still collect their pension.

"We set up a recruitment campaign targeted specifically for our retirees," says Lesley Mayer, RN, SPHR, manager of human resources. "At their first meeting about retiree benefits, we plant the seed. Six months later, we send them a letter saying, "We miss your expertise. Please come back and join the '1,000-Hour Club.'"[23]

the manager, and the department. Employee job performance should be a consideration in the determination of request approval. Expect adjustments to the initial plan to be needed for alternative work arrangements. Figure 3 provides a sample of the type of form that can be used to document requests for such arrangements.

Here are some of the options current near-retirement employees can be offered:

- Being loaned to other departments

- Taking a sabbatical or an active volunteer role in the community to gain and bring back specific experiences from outside the organization

- Participating on tiger teams formed specifically to solve issues and then returning to their full-time position

- Leading new efforts that represent the organization's future

- Trying a new arrangement: job sharing, working part-time, telecommuting, or working remotely

  Early retirees and retired alumni can take on the following roles:

- Re-trained returnee, full-time or part-time

- On-call employee to cover during lunch or dinner breaks

- Vacation back-up

- Adjunct staff member brought in during peak periods

- Consultant to guide long projects

- Project staff to serve as a peer to employees on projects

- Trainer or mentor to augment fundamental skills

- Boomerang hire at the manager level or above

## RETHINK RECRUITING

For years, we have said that organizations need to attract diverse candidates, create a pipeline of qualified talent for future hiring needs, and

**FIGURE 3 • SAMPLE REQUEST FORM**

## Alternative Work Schedule Request Form

Name: _____ Title: _____ Department: _____

Manager: _____ Exempt: Yes___ No___ (check one)

Desired option: Flextime ____ Job Sharing ____ Telecommuting ____

Compressed Work Week ____ Phased Retirement ____

Requested Start Date:
    Requested beginning _____ and ending _____ date

• • • •

Describe request: (include current schedule and needed change of hours, work location, or both)

How will this work alternative enhance your ability to perform your job?

What are potential scheduling or workload impacts and what options do you see that will address these issues?

Approval: _____ Date _____
           (Name and title)

Agreed: _____ Date _____
           (Associate)

---

### Engagement = Performance = Profits at IBM

In 2000, IBM senior management realized that while they had plenty of promising new business ideas, commercializing them was proving difficult. The most talented and experienced executives were running the old established businesses that accounted for current sales and profits, not the risky new efforts that represented future growth and profits. Launching new businesses became successful only after the company's president, Samuel J. Palmisano, recognized that the talent needed to run them could be found in his senior management ranks.

Rod Adkins was asked to move from running the UNIX computing division, with 35,000 employees and $4 billion in sales, to creating an emerging business opportunity (EBO) from scratch. His new venture—an application of wireless technology that extends computing beyond the home and office to, for example, cars with voice navigation systems—had $2.4 billion in sales at the end of three years! By applying his deep customer and organizational knowledge, Adkins vastly increased the odds of viability and speeded the profitability of the new venture.

Since 2000, IBM has launched twenty-five EBOs; twenty-two were successful and now generate more than $15 billion in revenue, a figure that is growing more than 40 percent per year. The big change is that IBM no longer relegates new business development to inexperienced people. Its senior managers tap their A-list of executives.[24]

---

provide a wow experience to applicants and candidates in order to stand out from their talent competition. The focus has been on fresh-faced new grads and other 20- to 40-year-old candidates from outside the organization. Today, diversity of candidates includes age, the candidate pipeline is both internal and external, and the wow experience is likely to include alternative work arrangements and other accommodations. Anything less will cause you to miss out on top performers who happen to be retired from their first or second career. For example, retired Purdue University French professor Sidney Pellisier, 68, reinvented himself as a certified personal trainer who also teaches weekly Body Pump, Pilates, and yoga classes. Of his seven to ten hours a week of working

> ### Engagement = Performance = Profits at E&Y and P&G
>
> Keeping the door open pays off. About 25 percent of Ernst & Young's manager and director hires are returning employees, according to Helen Walsh, director of recruiting and lifelong relationships. Re-hires frequently result from reunions attended by current and former employees.
>
> The Procter & Gamble Alumni Network has more than eight thousand members, many of whom have helped the company tackle business problems. "As large shareholders, it's in their best interest to help the company to be successful," says P&G alum and executive recruiter Ed Tazzia.[25]

out, he says, "You more than get back everything that you give in efficiency, and how you perform everything."[26]

The manager's role in hiring is more critical today than ever before. HR and hiring managers need to team up to develop more and different strategies and tactics to grab the attention of seasoned employees. This may mean that HR will need to educate managers who are uncomfortable with the idea of interviewing, hiring, and managing employees with more years of experience than they have. Today's seasoned candidate will be turned off by a hiring manager's ambivalence and will go to a talent competitor. Building up your managers' interview skills and increasing their generational comfort and knowledge levels will make the hiring process flow more positively.

Near-retirement and retiree candidates need to feel an immediate fit with your organization's employee value proposition (why they should work there) or employment brand (its reputation on the street for what it is like to work there). Why should this candidate work for you? How will your organization uniquely apply his or her skills, knowledge, and abilities?

The interview experiences of internal and external job candidates are a key element of your organization's employment brand. Every experience a job candidate has with your organization (advertising, Web site, speed of response, your preparation for the interview, timing between

---

### Engagement = Performance = Profits for Trucking Industry

A billboard and television ad campaign is just one of the strategies being used to attract older drivers to careers in the trucking industry. Faced with a serious shortage of long-haul truck drivers, freight carriers are aggressively recruiting the RV generation to climb into the cabs of their eighteen-wheelers. Another successful strategy has been to recruit husband-and-wife teams and to make the big rigs feel more like homes away from home. Paccar Inc.'s Kenworth Truck Co. unit introduced a model with leather beds and heated seats. Volvo Trucks North America now produces trucks with a full-size bed in the cab, so couples will be comfortable. Other tactics include recruiting through AARP and creating special corporate Web pages for "mature workers."

Drivers 55 to 69 have the lowest fatality rates for adults, according to a 2004 National Highway Safety Administration report. Once they qualify, couples find their new career taking them places they always dreamed of going.

Since 2000, the number of service and truck drivers over age 55 has surged 19 percent, according to the U.S. Bureau of Labor Statistics. After graduating from commercial driving school, all drivers must pass a physical exam—and there is no mandatory retirement age.[27]

---

interview and follow-up, receptionist's greetings, and chance "hellos" to talented potential peers) validates or refutes your organization's reputation as a terrific place to work. You want the best possible candidates beating down the door to work at your organization.

Every manager needs to team with HR to ensure that the following are up-to-date:

- **Job descriptions.** Job descriptions should include the competencies (combined skills and behaviors) of star performers. Specifying required competencies automatically eliminates average performers from the initial selection process, so this step should be integrated into the interview and reference checking processes. Make job descriptions available to all candidates.

- **Application media and processes.** Make it easy for internal and external candidates to use any medium to apply—Internet, fax, mail, in person, and so on. Ensure that internal candidates have a genuine opportunity to interview. Be responsive to questions and keep applicants informed if an appropriate job becomes available. Does your organization's Web site show photos of real employees of all ages? Does it mention the options for alternative work arrangements? Are organizational awards, employee community involvement activities, or client names shown? Is it possible to take initial skills assessments online? Can the applicant ask questions and get them answered in a timely manner?

- **Manager interview skills.** Ask HR to conduct or locate an interactive interview skills training program for all hiring managers. Interviewing longtime employees (your own or someone else's) may require extra skills to draw out achievements these workers have always felt were just part of the job. Alternatively, many seasoned candidates may feel more confident in an interview situation than does the hiring manager because they have been on that side of the desk, too. How well you and your managers interview candidates not only determines the quality of the ultimate hire, it also strongly influences the candidate's decision to join your team. To feel comfortable with more than one type of interview (phone, one-to-one, group) and with a variety of diverse candidates, have hiring managers practice interview skills with each other.

- **Quality interview questions.** Managers need to team with HR to develop a standard set of questions for each position in their department, giving special attention to positions that will be off-site or have nonstandard work arrangements. Focus on the candidate's values and invite the candidate to tell stories demonstrating his or her use of the competencies needed to be a star. Toward the end of the interview, consider adding three questions that may separate otherwise similar candidates:

  - "If I met your current or past manager at a social event, what would he or she tell me about you?"

- "How would you fill in this sentence: 'Every day, I come in to work prepared to _____'?"
- "Please tell me what three things will determine whether you accept an offer from us?"

Never hire a list of skills, a résumé, or an application. Hire the person who best fits your needs. Remember, every hire is a critical hire and fit with your department and projects is important.

- **Skills verification processes.** Team with HR to develop or select real-world tests to augment interview responses. For promising candidates, request that they do something relevant to the job:

  - **Skills tests.** These tests can be purchased or developed and might include math, writing, computer or engineering skills, and the like. Select skills appropriate to the position.

  - **Action plans.** Ask candidates to outline a marketing or sales plan or even a plan for their first thirty days on the job.

  - **Creative projects.** For candidates who must have strong writing or building skills, give an actual assignment with a realistic deadline.

  - **Presentations.** Ask top sales or trainer candidates to prepare a brief presentation for the next interview.

  - **Role-playing.** If appropriate, ask candidates to role-play scenarios with a difficult team member or customer, a first-time prospect, and so on. Another variation is an in-box exercise that demonstrates rapid decision making if needed on the job. Today's timed role-plays include paper and online elements to reflect the mix of media and deadlines typical on the job.

- **Psychological fit assessments.** Work with HR to choose an appropriate assessment for use in the final phases of interviewing. Assessments are intended to provide information that is otherwise difficult to uncover. While it is fairly easy to verify a candidate's hard skills, many employers want information about a person's psychological fit with the company, such as his or her truthfulness, team mind-set, or decision-making style. Bear in mind that each person's behavior is influenced by personality as well as environment (or organizational culture), so personal characteristics of the top performer in one organization or position are likely to differ from those of the top performer in another. Too much reliance on assessment results—or the use of a tool that does not measure appropriate characteristics—may needlessly screen out potentially successful employees. Use common sense even with well-known assessments when evaluating an individual.

- **Background checks.** No employer can afford to neglect background verification processes. Overstatement of experience, education, licenses, salary, or job titles is uncovered in 25 to 45 percent of background checks.[28] Employers can validate relevant information such as criminal record, social security number, employment history, education, driving record, credit history, worker's compensation claims, and civil court records. These checks may take as little as one to three days, but be patient whatever it takes; you don't want the liability and unpleasant publicity that can result from hiring frauds, illegal aliens, violent employees, and other undesirables.

- **Cultural fit.** The interview process is a mutual sales exercise. You have the open position, the training and development, the environment, the opportunity to work with talented peers, as well as the position's potential for advancement to sell to the candidate. The candidate has skills, energy, and aspirations to sell to the organization. The fewer qualified candidates available, the more it is a buyer's (candidate's) market. Everything that happens from the moment the candidate sets foot on your property sends a message about your organization's culture and the work experience that individual can expect.

A diverse workforce—including age diversity—is good business. Organizations that do the best job of communicating the diversity of their workforce are often the companies with the highest revenue share of their industries.[29]

---

### Engagement = Performance = Profits at Days Inn and Knights Inn

"It's a positive experience for us," says Dottie Justice, director of human resources for Parsippany, New Jersey–based Days Inn and Knights Inn. The benefits outweigh the disadvantages, and the myths about working with retirees are simply that: myths. Retirees who self-select to keep working are generally healthier than their nonworking counterparts, are just as capable of learning new computer skills as are younger workers, and adapt well to changes in working conditions or hours.

Approximately 10 percent of the 900-employee reservations department are seniors. "What seniors do best is give us a good work ethic," Justice adds. "They show up on time, and they care. They get to mentor young adults on the work ethics that we're really lacking in our workforce today."[30]

---

## RE-CREATE CAREER DEVELOPMENT

"Buy it or build it?" has been an organizational conundrum for many years as organizations have weighed the pros and cons of hiring versus developing talent. When skilled candidates were readily available, it was an easy decision: buy (hire) the needed skills. As recently as the late 1990s, entire departments of employees were shown the door and replaced with new hires with fresher skills. Even in the face of higher recruiting and compensation costs and the potential that these new hires would leave quickly if offered even more compensation elsewhere, hiring was considered the wiser choice because the new hires could immediately use new technologies.

Building (developing) skills in current employees as well as in second- and third-career job candidates has become a necessity as the speed of change continues to increase and there is more lag time between the availability of new technology and the availability of job candidates

---

**Engagement = Performance = Benefits for FHN—Again!**

"We know that retirement will hit health care especially hard," says Len Carter, vice president of human resources at FHN, a multiple award–winning regional health care system serving the needs of the people of northwest Illinois and southern Wisconsin. "We decided to make it easier for employees and nonemployees to train for second and third careers in medical fields."

Instead of waiting and hoping, FHN is building the workforce it needs. FHN has several initiatives that re-create traditional career development and fill the pipeline of future candidates by offering multiple channels for currently working individuals to acquire new degrees. Some of the options include funding instructors and developing an ADN (associate's degree in nursing) evening course in partnership with Highland Community College; offering fifteen scholarships for LPN, ADN, and RN (registered nurse) candidates; participating as the clinical site for an online lab technician training effort through a partnership with the Workforce Investment Board and Weber State University; and providing extensive scholarships for CNAs (certified nursing assistants) to get their LPN or RN degrees—including tuition, books, and fees for four years. Scholarship recipients are paid for eighty hours of work during a two-week pay period when they are actually going to school and working forty hours.[31]

---

trained to use it. Factor in the expected shortage of 800,000 to 3.3 million U.S. workers by 2010, and building skills is the only viable option.[32]

It is wise to make building skills rapidly and well a main feature of your organization. Building skills enables the development of proprietary skills that fit the culture, customer, and employee. The time and cost of recruiting can be traded or refocused on training existing employees. Career development is the number one attractor of top talent for an organization—and the number one element of engagement for current employees.

As demographics change and fewer talented individuals are available, most organizations will need to develop competencies as both buyers and builders of skills. No one-sided approach will work as the unemployment rate slides below 4 percent and competitors are beating on your best customer's door. If longtime employees have been neglected in the development area, they need to know they now have an opportunity to play a critical role in the future of the organization. But first, they'll need to polish their skill sets, and you'll need to help them.

## IT'S TIME FOR COORDINATED ACTION

Early and on-time retirements can be anticipated and plans made to minimize their negative effects. Attracting replacements will require a fresh view of who is a viable job candidate and what is a useful work arrangement. Internal candidates need to be recruited as never before. Future hires should include retirees—yours and your competition's—as well as future grads. Second- and third-career candidates are already becoming more common. As more 50-year-old new grads present themselves as candidates for hire, employers must consider the added value of their life and work experiences. In addition to fresh skills, the employer has the opportunity to hire the work habits, soft skills, judgment, and customer focus honed by years of experience. Expect to pay more—and get more performance, faster—from these new hires.

A confidential survey of your longtime employees will give you insight into their plans and your and their near-term needs. Go out of your way—way out of your way—to ensure the confidentiality of employee responses. Only if your employees feel totally assured of confidentiality will they participate honestly in the survey.

### Leverage Longtime Employees

- **For HR:** What is your organization's policy regarding the age of employee retirement? Is there a formula of age plus years of service that enables full or partial collection of retirement benefits? What percentage of your employees has already taken early retirement? If the trend continues, which functions will be most affected? Have recent retirees and early retirees been surveyed about what might have kept them on the job longer?

- **For senior management:** What is your organizational strategy? What types of knowledge are needed to ensure that goals are achieved? Are knowledge capture and transfer already part of your planning and actions? If not, a great source of information is David DeLong's *Lost Knowledge: Confronting the Threat of an Aging Workforce.*[33]

- **For managers and HR:** Are you ready for questions from second- and third-career job candidates? Do you know the percentage of employees over 50 in your organization? Is phased retirement available? Is age diversity training part of management and employee development? How much flexibility does your organization offer workers nearing retirement?

- **For all managers:** How can you encourage and reward aerobic activity and build in "neurobic exercises" to staff meetings and weekly activities? How can you reward and create accountability for improving employee brain function through simple actions? Could you have a competition for employees to develop simple actions to challenge themselves? Fight off the effects of physical and mental aging!

• • • •

6

# Create the Culture You Need Now

Keep America beautiful: don't litter your hallways with disengaged long-time employees and their ignored ideas. The opportunity cost is too high. Your biggest talent competitor is poised to pick up and recycle your best longtime employees as well as their ideas. You cannot afford to waste the minds, relationships, and deep knowledge of your most customer-focused, product-savvy, dedicated, near-retirement employees— or your retirees, either. Remember: change your expectations and you will change your results.

Does your organization have a culture of attendance—or a culture of performance? Do your performance management processes reward longevity—or innovation and creativity? Is everyone held accountable for listening to customers and responding with "Of course!" or "Let's talk about how to make this happen"?

Here is a quick test: If a 57-year-old employee were to have a brainstorm about a radical new product, would he or she get a shot at leading the project team? What if a retiree stopped by to suggest a way you could permanently cut operational costs. Would anyone listen? If a longtime employee were to suggest a way to meet an oddball customer request, would your managers say, "Try it"? If you answer no to any of these questions, it is time for a culture change. Create a culture that, instead of valuing input from only a select few, expects and cultivates ideas from everyone.

In the past, organizational cultures existed to prevent change. Today, your organization's culture must respond to customer-focused change by rewarding accountability, productivity, innovation, and creativity from all employees at all levels and of all ages.

Your marketplace is global and growing, thanks largely to the Internet. Your organization's future product, service, or even talent competition may not be your current product or service competition. You must keep quality and production high while experimenting with new avenues of products and services. Your customer wants something customized today and will want something customized differently tomorrow—without sacrificing quality or paying more.

To meet evolving customer needs, speed to innovation—not just in products and services but in internal processes—is critical today for

---

### Engagement = Performance = Profits at Google

At Google, everything about the culture encourages and rewards innovation. In three years, the company has launched an average of one product per week. Nearly all employees have the title of product manager. Employees are encouraged to propose wild, ambitious ideas, and supervisors assign small teams to test the ideas. Engineers are allotted 20 percent of their time to work on their own ideas. While Google places a premium on success, failure is shrugged off. The resulting culture of innovation and fearlessness permeates the air.

"If you are not failing enough, you are not trying hard enough," says Richard Holden, product management director. "The stigma [for failure] is less because we staff projects leanly and encourage them to just move on. If it doesn't work, move on."[1]

organizational growth and stability. The organizations with cultures that encourage listening, innovation, and creativity are in many ways the opposite of those that focus on quality and efficiency—yet we must have *all* these elements to satisfy our customers and stay competitive.

Your workforce demographics are changing by every measure: ethnic and religious mix, age and sexual distribution, and nation of origin, to name a few. But it is the change wrought by the retirement of longtime employees that can do the most damage to customer relationships and product and process knowledge, so this change must be controlled and minimized. The preference of longtime employees for alternative work arrangements and the desire of retirees to keep up their skills through part-time, seasonal, or project work are a perfect fit for today's work world.

Today, nearly every organization has a relatively fluid work environment and culture that includes teleworkers, employees at multiple sites, and virtual teams, with increased use of technology to maximize communication. Rapid job content additions and changes are common. There are fewer rigid job descriptions than in the past; instead, responsibilities are keyed to values, initiatives, and projects. Employees have learned to expect shorter tenure per position and promotability tied to performance rather than tenure. Many positions are project focused rather than rigid steps on a ladder.

In response to these and future changes, adaptable benefits will become more common. Training and participation in organizational events will be offered to more part-time employees. Adaptable compensation will become more common, too, including more frequently negotiated salary and wage increases, mini-raises at project end, spot bonuses, and increased use of rewards and recognition.

This chapter addresses how to develop a culture of performance and ongoing innovation while engaging and making the best use of all employees, especially knowledgeable near-retirement employees and retirees. The role of senior management, managers, and HR will be critical in making any culture change happen.

## YOU ARE THE CULTURE

According to the American Society for Training and Development, culture is "an organization's beliefs, knowledge, attitudes, and customs. Culture may result in part from senior managers' beliefs, but it also results from employees' beliefs. It can be supportive or unsupportive and positive or negative. It can affect employees' ability or willingness to adapt or perform well."[2]

You are the walking, talking culture of your organization as far as your direct reports are concerned. Whether you are in senior management, middle management, or human resources, employees look to you as a role model and values validator. You let them know what really matters through your attire, work space, praise, meeting start times, actions, word choice, and facial expressions. You model the organization's mission and values, rewarding or punishing employees for following or

---

### Engagement = Performance = Profits at Toyota, Georgetown

Toyota restructures itself a little bit every work shift. The company has an institutional obsession with improvement, which is instilled in every employee. There is a pervasive lack of complacency with whatever was accomplished yesterday. For Chad Buckner, engineering manager of the painting department, paint shop improvements aren't "projects" or "initiatives," they are the work itself—every day, every week, every year. Toyota does not make cars; it makes new ways to make cars.

As recently as 2004, it took ten hours and a hundred gallons of paint for robots to paint a car body at the Toyota plant in Georgetown, Kentucky. Cars had to be batched by color. Today the process takes eight hours and seventy gallons of paint. Using less paint requires using less cleaning solvent and has dramatically reduced disposal costs for both. Paint booths can now handle fifty cars an hour instead of thirty-three. "We are getting the same volume with two booths that we used to get with three, so we shut one down," says Buckner. The energy savings of shutting down an oven big enough to bake twenty-five cars is significant.[3]

breaking written or unwritten rules. Without seeing and hearing the values modeled by you, employees cynically experience the organization's values as nothing more than empty words.

If the culture is to change to truly value performance over attendance, innovation and creativity, quality and efficiency, and even the contributions of near-retirement employees and retirees, you must be the catalyst. Start by being open to change yourself. Change the rules, the rewards, the behaviors, and the goals. Rid yourself and your organization of the five myths covered in Chapter 3 that waste the potential contributions of much-needed longtime employees. Instead, put in place a culture based on expecting, rewarding, encouraging, enabling, and measuring outstanding performance—the five truths revealed in Chapter 4.

## IMPLEMENT POSITIVE CULTURE CHANGE

Culture change is a process, not an event. Leaders and their goals, and economic and demographic circumstances shape cultures. Today, we all have a world marketplace with worldwide competition. Instead of a large population of highly educated future employees waiting to be hired, our biggest pool of top talent can be found inside our organizations, among our longtime employees, and nearby, among recently retired individuals. Combined, these are the only growing segments of the employable population. The opportunity costs of disengaged long-term employees—half of most organizations' staffs—and disconnected retirees are too great to tolerate.

Seven steps can serve as a guide to creating the desired culture:

1. **Create and communicate a vision of an innovative organization with engaged employees of all ages and tenures.** Valuing the contributions and potential of all employees is the first step to ensuring the engagement of all employees. Accountability and recognition for innovation and creativity will motivate employees to contribute to the organization's success. Involve all generations in the organization's vision using all available channels of communication, and

provide opportunities for participation in establishing and maintaining the vision. Gen X and Gen Y employees—victims of ageism themselves—are strong proponents of basing rewards on competence and contribution rather than tenure.

2. **Connect the need for change to a desired business case and results.** Bias is a four-letter word. We have accepted age bias and other forms of bias for too long. Information—facts, data, and case studies—can be a strong motivator for change. All employees must understand the importance of the desired culture change and how it connects to the current culture that has brought the organization to this point. Repeatedly invite employees to articulate how the new culture has benefited or will benefit them as individuals as well as how it will enable sustained growth for the organization.

3. **Ensure that senior leaders as well as middle managers are committed to the process and will model the agreed-on behaviors.** Many organizations tie a portion of senior managers' variable pay to the achievement of specific goals in this area. Since senior leaders and middle managers are the walking, talking culture in the eyes of their employees, it is critical that they walk and talk the new desired culture. Anything less than total buy-in and myth busting will slow the process. Change-oriented leadership behaviors include measures such as these:

   - Challenging prevailing wisdom
   - Building new coalitions
   - Communicating the new goals repeatedly
   - Showcasing longtime employees and their accomplishments
   - Promoting longtime employees or giving them important assignments
   - Making heroes of those who step up to put changes in place

4. **Define the guiding behaviors that support the organization's values.** Specific performance outcomes are required to move the initiative forward. A time line with several preliminary goals is needed. For example, if employees past the up-and-comer stage have lower than

desired participation in brainstorming sessions, training, promotions, or project leadership, set goals for managers to increase levels in the next six months.

5. **Align support systems such as performance management, hiring and firing, training, and recognition to reinforce the desired culture.** Support systems ensure that the desired culture is initiated and perpetuated. If your goal is a workplace that values differences and the contributions of all employees, where is this goal documented in the hiring, assimilation, training, promotion, overall development, and reward processes and materials? Is it on your Web site? Is it a value that is part of your employment brand? Are there any negative consequences—up to and including firing—for those managers who do not value the full range of employees?

6. **Conduct a cultural audit before starting the effort and every six to twelve months thereafter to measure progress.** Employ external consultants who can ensure confidentiality, as that will make it more likely that you will receive truthful input.

7. **Work closely with HR leadership to craft the messages, media, and accountability for positive culture change.** Tap into the experiences of your own and other organizations' HR leaders to help plan and smooth the transition. Steep your HR staff in the business and its challenges and competitors. Ensure that HR is at the table for any planning or strategy meetings, and participates on any cross-functional teams. Involve HR in the development of new performance management systems and reward and recognition programs, as well as any new staffing requirements, action steps, and metrics. Expect HR staff at all levels to join with senior and middle management to model the new culture.

Culture change requires constant two-way, up-down communication and a critical mass to negate old behaviors. Each of the steps described must be taken for changes to succeed. True behavioral change occurs at the emotional level, not the intellectual level. Communicate regularly about successes along the way. Change hearts as well as minds, and the culture will more quickly reflect the new reality.

## IT'S TIME FOR COORDINATED ACTION

A positive culture that enables all employees—even those past the up-and-comer stage—to innovate and create will take your organization successfully into its infinite marketplace. Be proud of past accomplishments, but expect employees to listen deeply to their internal and external customers so that when the next request for customization or change occurs, it can happen smoothly. Aim for the moon every day. Never settle for "good enough."

---

### Leverage Longtime Employees

- **For all managers and HR:** In 2006, GM and Ford terminated 46,000 North American employees, while Toyota has never closed a north American factory—and in fact plans to open two new ones in 2007 and 2008. A typical Toyota assembly line operated in the United States makes thousands of operational changes a year, and its individual line employees change the way they work dozens of times a year. How much have you changed your work routine in the past year? In the past decade? What needs to change first?

- **For all managers and HR:** What does your organization really value? What are three words that describe your culture? What are three words that describe your desired and needed culture? What are you going to do to make innovation and creativity an expectation of every employee (including near-retirees who are on staff)?

- **For HR:** When was the last employee opinion survey or cultural audit conducted? Would a different survey provide better information for needed culture change? Consider resources such as www.gallup.com, www.walkerinfo.com, www.modernthink.com, and www.loyalty.com.

• • • •

---

# • • • • Epilogue

The war for talent has widened to become less a matter of recruiting new employees and more a quest to capture current employees' discretionary effort. Why bother with re-igniting the engagement and delaying the retirement of half of today's working population? In addition to the massive labor and skills shortages the impending Boomer retirement will cause, research shows that discretionary effort and the ROI—return on individual—from longtime A players with deep product, service, and customer knowledge can be significant. Towers Perrin's Global Workforce study shows that when employees believe they can reduce costs and improve customer satisfaction, it is much easier to achieve key business objectives.[1] The higher-quality work results of highly engaged employees are proof that we all—employees and management alike—get what we expect.

Too few employers are taking real action to create a work environment that will improve workforce performance and generate a competitive advantage. Specifically, too few in senior, middle, and HR management understand the wellspring of energy, ideas, and customer satisfaction highly engaged employees can provide. Only 25 percent of employers say they are ready for the mass exodus of knowledgeable employees. This is your opportunity! By taking action now, your organization can maximize the positive impact of retiring employees well before they go—and even after retirement. And workforce statistics illustrate that it's also a stark necessity:

- 40 percent of the Centers for Disease Control's 9,000 employees are eligible to retire in 2008.[2]

- The average machinist is well over age 50. Even now, before large-scale retirement hits, only 15,000 new machinists are entering the workforce annually to fill 45,000 openings.

- Currently, the nation faces a shortage of 250,000 math and science teachers. By 2016, 60,000 teachers are expected to retire in Indiana alone.[3]

- Today's U.S. nursing shortage is 200,000. By 2020, the shortage is expected to result in 800,000 to 1 million unfilled openings.[4]

- Half of all nuclear industry employees are age 47 or older and 23,000 retirements are expected by 2011, according to the Washington-based Nuclear Energy Institute. With fifteen new reactors expected to come online in the United States by 2015, aggressive action is needed to fill openings with experienced hires.[5]

- Cities are competing for college-educated workers between ages 25 and 34 to replace the Baby Boomers who are retiring and moving away.[6]

At a time of worldwide competition, "just doing the job" is not enough. So how do engaged longtime employees and even retirees use their discretionary effort to increase individual ROI? Table 4 gives the answer. It reveals an array of actions you can expect from truly engaged longtime employees and even retirees beyond just doing their job.

Because of the implications for the bottom line, boards of directors have begun to hold senior management responsible for low discretionary effort and low ROI. Current efforts tend to focus on up-and-

| TABLE 4 | HOW LONGTIME EMPLOYEES AND RETIREES INCREASE ROI | |
|---|---|---|
| **MEANS** | **LONGTIME EMPLOYEES** | **RETIREES** |
| **Reduce recruiting costs** | Refer high-quality internal and external candidates | Take on a project so you need not hire and orient an outside consultant |
| | Accept promotion | Work part-time, job-share, phase hours toward retirement |
| | Participate in ongoing training and 360-degree feedback | Return seasonally for part-time work |
| | Decline job offers | Accept on-call positions |
| **Reduce operational costs** | Contribute ideas | Contribute ideas |
| | Refer a vendor | Refer a vendor |
| **Reduce training costs and increase knowledge capture** | Document standard operating procedures and projects upon completion | Return to work to document processes and case studies |
| | Mentor Gen X, Y, and Z | Mentor |
| | Accept mentoring from Gen X, Y, and Z | Train others |
| **Reduce sales costs** | Provide the levels of customer service that result in repeat purchases and increased volume per customer | Become customers<br>Refer customers |

comers and high-potentials—yet an additional resource has been on board all along! What percentage of your current employees are near-retirement Baby Boomers and Veterans? How many retirees does your organization have? Senior, middle, and HR management need to start now to do the following:

- Analyze your current demographics and future skill needs
- Share your business plan with all employees
- Conduct baseline engagement surveys
- Train and reward managers for employee engagement
- Capture strategic knowledge
- Rethink recruiting, redefine retention, and reconstruct retirement
- Create a culture that thrives on customer-driven change
- Ask for input
- Expect excellence every day from every employee
- Reward risk taking and innovation
- Recognize all contributors
- Ignite your Boomer and Veteran power!

# • • • • Notes

## Chapter 1

1. "Watches and Clocks in the U.S.," 7th ed., by Packaged Facts, a research division of MarketResearch.com, July 1, 2006. Available online: www.packagedfacts.com/pub/1208059.html. Accessed: January 9, 2007.
2. "2005 Future of the U.S. Labor Pool: Survey Report," Society for Human Resource Management, 2005.
3. "Challenges Facing the American Workplace, Summary of Findings," *The Seventh Annual Workplace Report*, Employment Policy Foundation, 2002.
4. "Winning the New Talent Game," Deloitte Development LLC, 2005. Available online: http://www.deloitte.com/dtt/cda/doc/content/us_humancapital_talent-managementcss.pdf. Accessed: June 5, 2007.
5. "Gartner on Outsourcing, 2005," Gartner Inc., October 13, 2005.
6. Jeffrey Pfeffer, "The Hidden Cost of Outsourcing," *Business 2.0*, March 1, 2006.
7. "The Graying Planet Revisited." *Trends*, August 2005. Available online to subscribers: http://www.trends-magazine.com/trend.php/Trend/941/Category/45. Accessed: June 5, 2007.
8. "The Graying Planet Revisited."
9. "The Graying Planet Revisited."
10. Corporate Leadership Council, "Driving Employee Performance and Retention Through Engagement: A Quantitative Analysis of the Effectiveness of Employee Engagement Strategies." Washington, DC: Corporate Executive Board, 2004. Available online to members: www.corporateleadershipcouncil.com.

11. ISR, "Motivating Men and Women at Work: Relationships vs. Rewards," August 3, 2004. Available online with registration: www.isrsurveys.com.
12. ISR, "Creating Competitive Advantage from Your Employees: A Global Study of Employee Engagement" (white paper), 2004. Available online: http://www.isrinsight.com/pdf/insight/Engagement%20White%20Paper-US%20Singles.pdf. Accessed: June 7, 2007.
13. Corporate Leadership Council, "Engaging the Workforce: Focusing on Critical Leverage Points to Drive Employee Engagement." Washington, DC: Corporate Executive Board, 2004, p. vii. Available online to members: www.corporateleadershipcouncil.com.
14. Corporate Leadership Council, "Engaging the Workforce," p. 6.
15. Wilmar B. Schaufeli and Arnold B. Bakker, "Job Demands, Job Resources, and Their Relationship with Burnout and Engagement: A Multi-Sample Study," *Journal of Organizational Behavior 25,* no. 3 (2004): 293–315.
16. James K. Harter, Frank L. Schmidt, and Theodore L. Hayes, "Business-Unit-Level Relationship Between Employee Satisfaction, Employee Engagement, and Business Outcomes: A Meta-Analysis," *Journal of Applied Psychology 87,* no. 2 (2002): 268–279. See also Schaufeli and Bakker, "Job Demands, Job Resources, and Their Relationship with Burnout and Engagement."
17. Harter, Schmidt, and Hayes, "Business-Unit-Level Relationship Between Employee Satisfaction, Employee Engagement, and Business Outcomes."
18. James K. Harter, "Managerial Talent, Employee Engagement, and Business Unit Performance," *Psychologist-Manager Journal 4* (2000): 215–224.
19. ISR, "The People Factor," April 29, 2004. Available online with registration: www.isrsurveys.com.
20. Jim Shaffer, "Measurable Payoff: How Employee Engagement Can Boost Performance and Profits," *Communication World,* July 1, 2004, p. 22.
21. Harter, Schmidt, and Hayes, "Business-Unit-Level Relationship Between Employee Satisfaction, Employee Engagement, and Business Outcomes."
22. Shaffer, "Measurable Payoff," p. 22.

## Chapter 2

1. Margaret M. Blair, "New Ways Needed to Assess New Economy," *Los Angeles Times,* November 13, 2000, p. B7.
2. Ed Michaels, Helen Handfield-Jones, Beth Axelrod, *The War for Talent* (Boston: Harvard Business School Press, 2001).
3. Walker Information, "Walker Loyalty Report for Loyalty in the Workplace," a survey of more than 2,500 people working at companies fifty or more employees (Indianapolis, Indiana: Walker Information, 2005). News release available online: http://www.walkerinfo.com/what/loyaltyreports/studies/employee05/. Accessed: June 6, 2007.
4. Walker Information, "Walker Loyalty Report for Loyalty in the Workplace."
5. Walker Information, "Walker Loyalty Report for Loyalty in the Workplace."
6. MetLife Foundation/Civic Ventures, "New Face of Work Survey," conducted by Princeton Survey Research Associates International, June 2005. Available online: http://www.civicventures.org/publications/surveys/new-face-of-work.cfm.

7. Scott Cawood and Rita V. Bailey, *Destination Profit: Creating People-Profit Opportunities in Your Organization* (Mountain View, CA: Davies-Black Publishing, 2006).
8. Corporate Leadership Council, "Engaging the Workforce: Focusing on Critical Leverage Points to Drive Employee Engagement" (Washington, DC: Corporate Executive Board, 2004), p. 24. Available online to members: www.corporateleadershipcouncil.com.
9. Marcus Buckingham and Curt Coffman, *First, Break All the Rules* (New York: Simon & Schuster, 1999), p. 30.

**Chapter 3**

1. Daniel Kadlec, "The Marathon Generation," *Time,* June 26, 2006.
2. Kadlec, "The Marathon Generation."
3. David C. Forman, "Solving the Talent Paradox," *Human Capital,* November/December 2005, p. 12.
4. Bob Dylan, "Forever Young," *Planet Waves,* Columbia Records, 1974.
5. Bill Leonard, "Aging Baby Boomers Bring Age Bias to the Forefront," *HR News,* May 11, 2005. Available online: www.shrm.org/hrnews_published/archives/CMS_012572.asp. Accessed: January 12, 2007.
6. George Elsey, "Building Employee Engagement at Sensis," *Strategic HR Review,* January/February 2005, p. 16.
7. "Ford Taps Employees for Ideas," *Detroit Free Press,* January 17, 2006.
8. MSN Money Staff, "Ford: 38,000 Workers to Leave," November 29, 2006. Available online: http://articles.moneycentral.msn.com/Investing/Extra/FordWorkersToLeave.aspx. Accessed: January 12, 2007.
9. Fiona Hadley, "Mutual Benefit," *Fast Company,* October 2004, p. 98.

**Chapter 4**

1. Daniel Kadlec, "A Car Salesman You Can Trust," *Time,* July 31, 2006, p. 67.
2. Martin Kasindorf, "Retired Sleuths Heat Up Cold Cases," *USA Today,* August 8, 2006, p. 3A.
3. Robert King, "In Their Words," *Indianapolis Star,* August 5, 2006, p. B5.
4. Jennifer Deal, "Learning and Development: Same or Different?" *CCL Newsletter,* February 2005: "Generations at Work." Available online with registration: http://www.ccl.org/leadership/enewsletter/2005/
5. Theresa Minton-Eversole, "Survey: Many Retirees Take Knowledge, Skill with Them When They Go," *EMA Forum News,* May 2005.
6. Ed Michaels, Helen Handfield-Jones, and Beth Axelrod, *The War for Talent* (Boston: Harvard Business School Press, 2001).
7. Bill Leonard, "Gallup: Workplace Bias Still Prevalent," *HR Magazine,* February 2006, p. 34.
8. Laurie T O'Brien and Mary Lee Hummert, "Memory Performance of Late Middle-Aged Adults: Contrasting Self-Stereotyping and Stereotype Threat Accounts of Assimilation to Age Stereotypes," *Social Cognition,* June 2006, p. 338.
9. Benedict Carey, "Memory Lapses May Be Self-Induced, Study Shows," *Indianapolis Star,* July 23, 2006, p. A24.

10. Carey, "Memory Lapses May Be Self-Induced, Study Shows."
11. R. H. Franke and J. D. Kaul, "The Hawthorne Experiments: First Statistical Interpretation," *American Sociological Review 43* (1978): 623–643.
12. J. Sterling Livingston, "Pygmalion in Management," *Harvard Business Review*, September/October 1988.
13. According to mythology, Pygmalion created Galatea as a statue of a "perfect woman" and fell in love with her. He asked the gods to make her human and they lived happily ever after.
14. Jeffrey K. Liker, *The Toyota Way* (New York: McGraw-Hill, 2003).
15. Ted Evanoff, "Back to the Factory," *Indianapolis Star*, September 3, 2006, p. D1.
16. Pamela Babcock, "Detecting Hidden Bias," *HR Magazine*, February 2006, p. 51.
17. Stephen Miller, "Employees Need Recognition," *SHRM Conference Daily*, June 21, 2005, p. 12.
18. Thad Green, *Motivation Management* (Mountain View, CA: Davies-Black Publishing, 2000), p. 66.
19. Bruce Tulgan, *FAST Feedback* (Amherst, MA: HRD Press, 1999), p. 86.
20. Gina Imperato, "How to Give Good Feedback," *Fast Company*, August 1998.
21. Walker Information, "Walker Loyalty Report for Loyalty in the Workplace," a survey of more than 2,500 people working at companies with fifty or more employees. (Indianapolis, IN: Walker Information, 2005). News release available online: http://www.walkerinfo.com/what/loyaltyreports/studies/employee05/. Accessed: June 6, 2007.
22. Walker Information, "Walker Loyalty Report for Loyalty in the Workplace."
23. Conference Board, "Most CEOs Say Flexibility and Adapting to Change Now Vital to Competing Worldwide" (press release), November 29 2004. Available online: www.conference-board.org/utilities/pressDetail.cfm?press_ID–2525. Accessed: January 15, 2007.
24. Charles Fishman, "How Many Light Bulbs Does It Take to Change the World? One," *Fast Company*, September 2006, pp. 75–83.
25. Michelle Conlin, "Champions of Innovation," *Business Week*, June 2006, p. IN19.
26. Conlin, "Champions of Innovation."
27. Myrna Marofsky and Ann Johnson, *Getting Started with Mentoring* (Minneapolis, MN: Ambassador Press, 2001).
28. John B. Horrigan, "A Typology of Information and Communication Technology Users" (Washington, DC: Pew Internet and American Life Project, May 7, 2007). Available online: http://www.pewinternet.org/pdfs/PIP_ICT_Typology.pdf. Accessed: June 6, 2007.
29. Cindy Krisher Goodman, "Older Workers Tap into Gen Y Savvy," *Seattle Times*, May 28, 2006, p. I1

## Chapter 5

1. Marshall Loeb, "Older Workers Often Struggle to Find Jobs That Suit Needs," *Contra Costa Times*, October 6, 2006.
2. Christopher Boyd, "Boomers' Exit Spells Work-Force Shortage," *Orlando Sentinel*, October 16, 2006, p. A1.
3. "Managers Regret One in Five New Hires," *Staffing Management*, April–June 2005, p. 13.

4. "2005 Future of the U.S. Labor Pool: Survey Report," Society for Human Resource Management, 2005.

5. "Older Workers: Untapped Assets for Creating Value," Knowledge@Wharton, February 9, 2005. Available online to subscribers: http://knowledge.wharton.upenn.edu/article.cfm?articleid–1123.

6. "The Graying Planet Revisited." *Trends*, August 2005. Available online to subscribers: http://www.trends-magazine.com/trend.php/Trend/941/Category/45. Accessed: June 5, 2007.

7. "The Graying Planet Revisited."

8. Theresa Minton-Eversole, "Survey: Many Retirees Take Knowledge, Skill with Them When They Go," *EMA Forum News*, May 2005.

9. Daniel Kadlec, "The Marathon Generation," *Time*, June 26, 2006.

10. M. L. Lengnick-Hall, P. Gaunt, and J. Collison, "Employer Incentives for Hiring Individuals with Disabilities Survey," *HR Magazine*, April 2003.

11. Barbara Lippert, "Truth in Advertising," *AARP Magazine*, November–December 2006, p. 14.

12. William D. Novelli, "Hiring Older Workers Is Good Business," *AARP Bulletin*, September 6, 2006, p. 31.

13. Towers Perrin, "Employers Are Creating a 'Culture of Health' to Balance Cost and Talent," *Towers Perrin Perspectives*, May 31, 2006. Available online: www.towersperrin.com/tp/getwebcachedoc?webc–HRS/USA/2006/200605/HW_culture.pdf. Accessed: January 20, 2007.

14. Watson Wyatt Worldwide, "Staying @ Work," 2005/2006, p. 4.

15. Watson Wyatt Worldwide, "Staying @ Work," p. 5.

16. Towers Perrin, "Employers Are Creating a 'Culture of Health' to Balance Cost and Talent."

17. Sharon Begley, "How to Keep Your Aging Brain Fit: Aerobics," *Wall Street Journal*, November 16, 2006, p. D1.

18. Lawrence Katz and Manning Rubin, *Keep Your Brain Alive: 83 Neurobic Exercises* (New York: Workman, 1998).

19. Allison Rossett and Jeannette Gautier-Downes, *A Handbook of Job Aids* (San Francisco: Pfeiffer, 1991), p. 45.

20. "Managing Knowledge for the New Economy" *IST Results*, October 12, 2006. (Publication available from Office BU31 01/19 B-1049 Brussels, Belgium.)

21. AARP's Best Employers for Workers Over 50," *AARP Magazine*, November/December 2004. Available online: http://www.aarpmagazine.org/lifestyle/Articles/a2004-09-22-mag-bestchart.html. Accessed: June 6, 2007.

22. Interview with Len Carter, vice president of human resources, FHN, Freeport, Illinois, November 8, 2006.

23. Pamela Babcock, "Savvy Companies Take Initiatives to Keep Experienced Workers," *Recruiting & Staffing News*, September, 2006. Available online to members of the Society for Human Resource Management: www.shrm.org/ema/news_published/CMS_018652.asp.

24. Alan Deutschman, "Building a Better Skunk Works," *Fast Company*, March 2005, p. 69.

25. Barbara Rose, "Alumni: New Style Networkers," *Chicago Tribune*, January 3, 2006.

26. Kevin Cullen, "Retired Professor Pumping Iron," *Indianapolis Star*, November 5, 2006, p. B5.

27. Stephanie Chen, "Over-50s Going Over the Road: Trucking Firms Recruit Older Drivers to Run Big Rigs," *Wall Street Journal*, August 28, 2006, p. C4.

28. Margaret Steen, "Employers Delve More Deeply into Workers' Pasts," *Indianapolis Star*, May 8, 2002, p. B7.

29. Kipp Cheng, "McDonalds Website Golden on Diversity," *DiversityInc*, May 24, 2002.

30. Diane Cyr, "Lost and Found—Retired Employees," *Personnel Journal 75*, no. 11 (1996): 40–47.

31. Interview with Len Carter, November 8, 2006.

32. Bill Leonard, "Aging Baby Boomers Bring Age Bias to the Forefront," *HR News*, May 11, 2005. Available online: www.shrm.org/hrnews_published/ archives/ CMS_012572.asp. Accessed: January 20, 2007.

33. David W. DeLong, *Lost Knowledge: Confronting the Threat of an Aging Workforce* (New York: Oxford University Press, 2004).

**Chapter 6**

1. Sara Kehaulani Goo, "At Google, It's All About Effort," *Indianapolis Star*, October 29, 2006, p. D1.

2. See the glossary to Laurie Bassi's "Harnessing the Power of Intellectual Capital," *Training & Development*, December 1997. Available online: www.astd.org/astd/ Resources/performance_improvement_community/Glossary.htm. Accessed: January 22, 2007.

3. Walker Information, "Walker Loyalty Report for Loyalty in the Workplace," a survey of more than 2,500 people working at companies with fifty or more employees. (Indianapolis, IN: Walker Information, 2005). News release available online: http://www.walkerinfo.com/what/loyaltyreports/studies/employee05/. Accessed: June 6, 2007.

**Epilogue**

1. Towers Perrin, "Global Workforce Study," HR Services, August 2005. www.TowersPerrin.com.

2. Christine Gorman, "What Ails the CDC?" *Time*, November 27, 2006, p. 61.

3. Staci Hupp, "Who'll Teach Our Children?" *Indianapolis Star*, March 12, 2006, p. A1.

4. Donald M. Atwater and Aisha Jones, "Preparing for a Future Labor Shortage," *Journal of Contemporary Business Practices* (Pepperdine University) 7, no. 2 (2004).

5. Hyan Young Lee, "Aging Workforce Poses Nuclear-Power Challenge," *Wall Street Journal*, April 11, 2006, p. A12.

6. Shaila Dewan, "Cities Covet Young Workers," *Indianapolis Star*, November 30, 2006, p. A4.

# • • • • Index